Boston, 135 Washington Street,
May, 1850.

NEW BOOKS AND NEW EDITIONS
PUBLISHED BY
Ticknor, Reed, and Fields.

MR. LONGFELLOW'S POEMS.

MR. LONGFELLOW'S COMPLETE POETICAL WORKS. This edition contains the six volumes mentioned below, and is the only complete collection in the market. In two volumes, 16mo, $2.00.

In separate Volumes, each 75 cents.

I.

THE SEASIDE AND THE FIRESIDE.

II.

EVANGELINE; A TALE OF ACADIE.

III.

VOICES OF THE NIGHT.

IV.

BALLADS AND OTHER POEMS.

V.

SPANISH STUDENT. A Play in Three Acts.

VI.

BELFRY OF BRUGES AND OTHER POEMS.

VII.

THE WAIF. A Collection of Poems. Edited by LONGFELLOW.

VIII.

THE ESTRAY. A Collection of Poems. Edited by LONGFELLOW.

MR. LONGFELLOW'S PROSE WORKS.

I.

KAVANAGH. A TALE. Lately Published. In one volume, 16mo, price 75 cents.

II.

OUTRE-MER. A PILGRIMAGE BEYOND THE SEA. In one volume, 16mo, price $1.00.

III.

HYPERION. A ROMANCE. In one volume, 16mo, price $1.00.

POETRY.

I.

OLIVER WENDELL HOLMES. Poems. In one volume, 16mo. New Edition, Enlarged. Price $1.00.

II.

CHARLES SPRAGUE. Poetical and Prose Writings. New and Revised Edition. With fine Portrait. In one volume, 16mo, price 75 cents.

III.

JAMES RUSSELL LOWELL. Complete Poetical Works. Revised, with Additions. In two volumes, 16mo, price $1.50.

IV.

JOHN G. WHITTIER. Songs of Labor and Other Poems. In one volume, 16mo. (Just ready.)

V.

EPES SARGENT. Songs of the Sea, with Other Poems. In one volume, 16mo, price 50 cents.

VI.

JOHN G. SAXE. Humorous and Satirical Poems. In one volume, 16mo, price 50 cents.

VII.

ROBERT BROWNING. Complete Poetical Works. In two volumes, 16mo. Price $2.00.

VIII.

ALFRED TENNYSON. Poems. A New Edition. Enlarged, with Portrait. In two volumes, 16mo, price $1.50.

IX.

ALFRED TENNYSON. The Princess. A Medley. In one volume, 16mo, price 50 cents.

X.

WILLIAM MOTHERWELL. Poems, Narrative and Lyrical. A New Edition, Enlarged. In one volume, 16mo, price 75 cents.

XI.

WILLIAM MOTHERWELL. Minstrelsy, Ancient and Modern. With an HISTORICAL INTRODUCTION and NOTES. In two volumes, 16mo, price $1.50.

XII.

RICHARD MONCKTON MILNES. Poems of Many Years. In one volume, 16mo, price 75 cents.

XIII.

PHILLIP JAMES BAILEY. Author of "Festus." THE ANGEL WORLD and OTHER POEMS. In one volume, 16mo. price 50 cents.

XIV.

LEIGH HUNT. Story of Rimini and Other Poems. In one volume, 16mo, price 50 cents.

XV.

REJECTED ADDRESSES. From the 19th London Edition. Carefully Revised. With an ORIGINAL PREFACE and NOTES. By HORACE and JAMES SMITH. In one volume, 16mo, price 50 cents.

XVI.

BARRY CORNWALL. ENGLISH SONGS and other SMALL POEMS. In one volume, 16mo, price 75 cents.

XVII.

JOHN BOWRING. MATINS AND VESPERS, with HYMNS AND OCCASIONAL DEVOTIONAL PIECES. In one volume, 32mo, cloth, gilt edges, price 37 1-2 cents.

EACH OF THE ABOVE POEMS AND PROSE WRITINGS, MAY BE HAD IN VARIOUS STYLES OF HANDSOME BINDING.

MISCELLANEOUS.

I.

ALDERBROOK. A Collection of Fanny Forester's VILLAGE SKETCHES, POEMS, etc. In two volumes, 12mo, with a fine Portrait of the Author. A New Edition, Enlarged. Just out. Price $1.75.

II.

GREENWOOD LEAVES. A Collection of GRACE GREENWOOD'S Stories and Letters. In one volume, 12mo. New Edition. Price $1.25.

III.

NATHANIEL HAWTHORNE. THE SCARLET LETTER. A ROMANCE. In one volume, 16mo, price 75 cents.

IV.

HORACE MANN. A FEW THOUGHTS FOR A YOUNG MAN. In one volume, 16mo, price 25 cents.

V.

EDWIN P. WHIPPLE. LECTURES ON SUBJECTS CONNECTED WITH LITERATURE AND LIFE. In one volume, 16mo. Just published. Price 63 cents.

VI.

JOHN G. WHITTIER. OLD PORTRAITS AND MODERN SKETCHES. In one volume, 16mo. Just published. Price 75 cents

VII.

JOHN G. WHITTIER. MARGARET SMITH'S JOURNAL. In one volume, 16mo. Price 75 cents

VIII.

HENRY GILES. LECTURES, ESSAYS, AND MISCELLANEOUS WRITINGS. Two volumes, 16mo. Price $1.50.

IX.

HENRY GILES. CHRISTIAN THOUGHT ON LIFE. In Twelve Discourses. (Nearly ready.)

X.

THE BOSTON BOOK FOR 1850. BEING SPECIMENS OF METROPOLITAN LITERATURE. In one volume, 12mo, price $1.25.

XI.

CHARLES SUMNER. ORATIONS AND SPEECHES. In two volumes, 16mo.

XII.

HEROINES OF THE MISSIONARY ENTERPRIZE. BEING MEMOIRS OF DISTINGUISHED AMERICAN FEMALE MISSIONARIES. In one volume, 16mo, price 75 cents.

XIII.

F. W. P. GREENWOOD. SERMONS OF CONSOLATION. A New Edition, on very fine paper and large type. In one volume, 16mo, price $1.00.

XIV.

CHARACTERISTICS OF WOMEN: MORAL, POETICAL and HISTORICAL. By MRS. JAMESON. New Edition, Corrected and Enlarged. In one volume, 12mo, price $1.00.

XV.

BEN PERLEY POORE. THE RISE AND FALL OF LOUIS PHILIPPE, with Pen and Pencil Sketches of his Friends and his Successors. Portraits. $1.00

XVI.

ANGEL-VOICES; or WORDS OF COUNSEL FOR OVERCOMING THE WORLD. In one volume, 18mo. A New Edition, Enlarged. Price 38 cents.

XVII.

THE CONSTITUTION OF MAN; Considered in Relation to External Objects. By GEORGE COMBE. With an Additional Chapter, on the HARMONY BETWEEN PHRENOLOGY AND REVELATION. By J. A. WARNE, A. M. Twenty-seventh American Edition. In one volume, 12mo, price 75 cents.

XVIII.

A PRACTICAL TREATISE ON THE CULTIVATION OF THE GRAPE VINE ON OPEN WALLS. To which is added, a Descriptive Account of an Improved Method of Planting and Managing the Roots of Grape Vines. With Plates. In one volume, 12mo, price 62 1-2 cents.

XIX.

ORTHOPHONY; Or the Culture of the Voice in Elocution. A Manual of ELEMENTARY EXERCISES, adapted to Dr. Rush's "PHILOSOPHY OF THE HUMAN VOICE," and the system of Vocal Culture introduced by Mr. James E. Murdoch. Designed as an INTRODUCTION to Russell's "AMERICAN ELOCUTIONIST." Compiled by WILLIAM RUSSELL, author of "Lessons in Enunciation," etc. With a Supplement on PURITY OF TONE, by G. J. WEBB, Professor, Boston Academy of Music. Improved Edition. In one volume, 12mo, price 62 1-2 cents.

XX.

MRS. PUTNAM'S RECEIPT BOOK; AND YOUNG HOUSEKEEPER'S ASSISTANT. A New and Enlarged Edition. In one volume, 16mo, price 50 cents.

XXI.

LIGHTS AND SHADOWS OF DOMESTIC LIFE. In one volume, 16mo. (Just ready.)

CHRISTIAN THOUGHT ON LIFE.

CHRISTIAN THOUGHT

ON LIFE.

IN A SERIES OF DISCOURSES.

BY

HENRY GILES,

AUTHOR OF "LECTURES AND ESSAYS."

BOSTON:
TICKNOR, REED, AND FIELDS.
MDCCCL.

BOSTON:
THURSTON, TORRY & COMPANY, PRINTERS,
DEVONSHIRE STREET.

PREFACE.

These Discourses were not written in pastoral relations, or for pastoral purposes. The general intention which governed in the composition of the greater number, was to gather into compact form, fragments of moral experience, and to give some record and some order to desultory studies of man's interior life. The author, therefore, not pressed by occasions which compel brevity, followed as he was moved the promptings of his feelings and his theme. Thus much the author ventures to advance as an apology for their length, beyond the measure commonly allowed to sermons.

Boston, July 1, 1850.

CONTENTS.

CHRISTIAN THOUGHT ON LIFE.

THE WORTH OF LIFE.

James, iv. 4.

FOR WHAT IS YOUR LIFE?

Complaints of the world and of life we often hear, even from those who have no rugged portion in both the world and life. The world is good; for it is God's world, made by his power, fashioned by his wisdom, and fitted by his bounty for many precious uses. The world is good, for it is man's world, the first home of his being, and the school of his destiny. Life is also good; for it is God's life, derived from his spirit and educated by his Providence, and formed for an existence imperishable and progressive. Life is good; for it is man's life, mighty in its capacities, mighty in purposes, and endowed with tender and sublime affections, great in their cultivation, and great in their exercise.

The ascetic view of life is, in its own way, as wrong as the sensual. The ascetic imagines that he can gain the future by despising the present. The sensualist fancies that he secures the present by contempt for the future. Each commits a radical mistake; each makes a partial estimate of life, and each in his error narrows and impoverishes it. The present contains the future, for the future is but the present that is to come; the future contains the present, for the future will be but a modification of what the present has been. Let ours be the Christian view of life; in which both the present and future are discerned to be but one life, — one in essence and one in interest. And according to this, by its light and teachings, let us proceed to inquire the value of life.

Life is a great fact. We live. Here is a momentous verity. Most mysterious, and yet most real, is this solemn *now*. We live, and some few years since, we were not. Out of the dread, dark, speechless abyss of possibilities, we have come to be among the things which are to move, to breathe. Before us lies the immense unknown, and deep silence is its covering. *We live*, and in that, is profound import: we feel, we think, we act. We have senses; we hear, see; we have affections; we have passions; we love, we ask for love, we desire, we hope, we fear, we are angry, we are pleased, we grieve, we are glad ; we have intellect ; we apprehend, we speculate, we remember, we reason, we believe, we imagine ; we see visions, and we dream dreams. We have conscience, we are formed for enjoyment in virtue, and not less for misery in sin. We have religious sentiment : we seek for God, we trust, we reverence, we worship ; we have withal the faculty of doing ; we translate ideas into deeds ; cause will to come forth in power, and power to exist in results.

What a sacred thing in its completeness, is an hour of human life, containing, as it seems, the elements of all other life. Mere sensation is grateful, and to feel being even in *that*, is a privilege. To breathe the air, to look upon the light, to hear the voice of nature in her countless tones, to rest upon her fragrant lap, and to be conscious of a beating pulse, this, low as it seems, is not unworthy of desire. But when existence is glorified with the perception of beauty, with the sentiment of grandeur, with the radiance of fancy, with the graces of culture ; when it is cheered by the warmth of friendship, by the sweetness of affection ; by the associations of memory ; by all that stirs within a kindred and a loving humanity ; when it is sanctified, moreover, by the sacred convictions of religion, it is of worth unutterable.

If it is precious to know existence, even in our instincts, how excellent to know it in our most godlike capacities. We *live*, and if our nature be to any extent active, vital, how vast is the range of our life. Our existence, to us involves the existence of creation. The present hour is not to me the hour of an isolated being. It is the hour of the earth which bears me on its surface. It is the hour of the heavens which stand over me with their unpillared canopy, which enfold me in an ocean of infinite glory and infinite light. It is the hour of all, my sentient fellow-creatures, in every region and every element, which move with myself in the world of pleasure and of pain. It is the hour of my friends, to whom my first sympathies are given, and from whom sympathies come to me in turn. It is the hour of my whole human brotherhood, — with every movement of my heart; the vibrations of a thousand millions keep time, and all the mysteries of life are within them, with all the varieties of sorrow and satisfaction. What a worth is therefore even in *this* hour, if indeed, it is an hour of life, not one of apathy, nor yet one of confusion. What worth, I repeat, in a single hour of true life! The worth of all that we perceive, of all that we feel, of the gracious earth, of the blessed heavens, of immeasurable vitality, of loving friends, of universal brotherhood. True, that material things existed before us, and without us. Once, they were alone with their God; the earth had no habitable places, the sunshine was not glad in human dwellings, the stars guided no mariner upon the seas; old ocean roared, but no man heard, no brave voices mingled with the noise of waters, deep called unto deep, and had only deep to answer. So it was, before there was an Adam, but man was created, and all things *lived.* And these now live to us, and besides these, all which the sons of Adam have wrought, language, learning, arts, cities, with their adornments, governments with their laws, and whatever else, the contrivance of man's head and the cunning of his hand have enabled him to do. Surely, even our present life is sacred, and is grand.

I have said, then, not untruly, that life is a great fact. It is also a fact with great relations. Nothing is separate in the creation or the providence of God, all things are connected, all have reference to each other, and to the whole. No existence is complete in itself but One, which is infinite and eternal. Others have all reference to each other and to that; and the laws of mind have no less a subordination and dependence than the laws of matter. The present day of our intelligent and moral existence, concentrates results from our past life. Impressions, thoughts, imaginations, desires, memories, pursuits, studies. Whatsoever entered into our experience, or shaped it, tended, each in its degree, to produce every moment of our existence as it comes. But the past, to which our present has relation, is not confined within our own experience, — it goes back beyond history, it enters into the mysterious era of unwritten revelation. Modes and habits which are now unconscious to us, are creatures of centuries. The simplest phrases of our common speech, have been ages in attaining their present articulation. Christian childhood, the Sunday-school, ministry to the poor, numberless other phases of life, have relation to a cross, which, eighteen hundred years ago, was raised on Calvary, in the remote province of Judea.

And thus it is with the distant as with the past. Not only do our relations of charity bind us to all regions of the world, but even those of covetousness and those of comfort. Wisdom and wealth come to us from afar, and our most ordinary and constant needs, many soils and many regions contribute to supply. And, by this law of continuity, the inevitable law of our spiritual being, the moments in which we now exist are bound to the future, and have their influence in determinining its character. What we *are* to be, is to be decided by what we have been and by what we are. So far as the principles operate, which we deduce from general experience, this is our inference. These laws of relationship belong to the present life; to the present day, the present hour. They belong to the being which we *now* have. The being which we have *now*, is that which we can have at any time. No other is to be ours, forever. Modified this may be, changed in its condition or its circumstances, but in spirit and in essence it must be the same; for the continuance of the individual is simply the identity of life. In this very hour even our immortality is included. For what is our immortality? What but the unfolding of that being which is already in us? Immortality is not something added: it is not a thing separate from us; it is in our souls; it is this moment in the action of every thought; it is ours now, and we have not to wait for it. The life which we hold while the minute-hand of a clock passes over its smallest interval, is that life, be it expanded how it may, which eternal duration will not exhaust.

Solemn, indeed, are these relations of our life; and solemn are the objects and the activities to which they bind us. God is the supreme object, in whom and by whom we are, in every movement and in every instant; God, the beginning and supporter of every being, the source of existence and its end. And then, how many are our associations with man, in kindred, in sympathy, in country, in species; by interchange, by co-operation, by community: community of thought, community of feeling, community of labor. What a host of obligations are involved in life, in order to preserve the harmony of its relations; the obligation to discipline, to train it into strength; the obligation to duty, which is the law of its perfection; the obligation to work, which is involved in both its wants and its capacities, an implied condition of its existence. And this work has no measure, but that of our sphere and that of our power; it begins with capability, and only with capability it concludes. When we walk forth on earth, *then* begins our labor; and our toil is not over, until that warning comes which tells the strong, equally with the feeble, that their day is closed. The field for some is bounded by the straitened circle of daily necessity; that of others embraces many regions, with a return of good fruit which will be bounty for many ages; but, large or limited, our life involves a work, and the purpose of our life is to do it. We contract this debt with life, and we owe it to all things and beings: we owe it for all excellence and all good; we owe it to the earth which feeds us; we owe it to the animals which help us; we owe it to God and man — to the dead and to the living;

to the dead, into whose labors we have entered, and to the living, whose labors we share.

Connected, therefore, with the life which now is ours, we find the relations that endow it with a solemn grandeur: those relations with the past, the distant, and the future; with our Creator and our brethren, with goodness and with action — those relations which constitute the dignity of beings. These all belong to our present life: they are parts of it; with that which is to be, they are possible; but with that which is, they are actual. If there be worth in these, then there is countless worth in every hour which we fill with the consciousness of a complete human existence. And I do not mean that our whole being should be concentred in the hour, but merely that the hour be complete in itself, and be sufficient for any true purpose of life; then it is the hour, not of a passive clod, but of a living soul.

Life is a fact involving great results. What is that which has been a power in human concerns, that did not come out of the life of man? Take that most stupendous life, or the little fragment of it which was visible to the world — that life which has re-moulded society — the life of Jesus Christ, — say whether it was not once a *present*, *actual* thing. Consider Jesus Christ theologically as we may, his influence upon life has been in the relations of humanity. Miracles may have startled sleeping faculties, and called attention to his mission; but it was moral being made manifest in action, that put a quickening spirit into the gross and dormant heart of our species. Miracles were but the accidents of his office: they had no necessary connection with the essence of his character. This character, as men recognise and feel it, is the same in its spiritual attributes; place Christ in what order of being they choose, when once they take him from the sphere of earth.

I speak of Christ's character as it was developed in a human life. Now, all that has been since done in the world, and all that is to be done in the world, while it endures, by the impulse of that life, were then involved in its passing deeds and speech. You know what a change has been effected in humanity by the influences of our Saviour's life; you know to what an extent this change has gone through the earth; you know how profoundly, how widely, how thoroughly, it has operated on opinion, on faith, on sentiment, on manners, on conduct, on worship, and on government. You have evidence of such before the senses, and within the heart; you have evidence of such, in every village church which gleams through the wood, or shines upon the hill; you have it in every rural school where childhood finds reverence and instruction; you have it in the sanctity of humble homes; you have it in the peace of Sabbath congregations; you have it in plans of mercy; you have it in dispensations of charity,—in an opulence of good works; you have it in amelioration of laws, in the dissemination of freedom; you have it in the holy strength which can bear suffering with humility, and which can encounter death with hope. And yet, the whole of those mighty results have flowed from a life which was short in years; only the close of which has been recorded, and even that but briefly in disjointed memoirs. A life thus prolific in consequences, was far from the centre of culture or of power. Unseen by the studious, and unknown to the great, it had its converse mainly with the poor, and its end with the infamous. Yet, see how that life has not only ruled events, but converted souls. It has regenerated intellect and affections; and of the millions which have been born again by its spirit, of the millions which have had a new creation by its energy, each intellect has found an aspect of it, original to its own view, an aspect its own, by individual observing and individual appropriation; each heart has discovered an attraction special to its own love, and to its own endearment.

This, as I have said, was once a *present*, *actual*, life

on earth; a life among men; a life spent much in cities, on highways, and not inconsiderably in a joiner's workshop. Will it be called presumption to adduce the life of Christ in connection with our life? If it be presumption, it is presumption which the apostle teaches, when he tells that Christ left us an example that we should follow his steps. But we think too meanly of our life, and thence its barrenness. We take a low standard, thence the lowness of our aimings, and thence, the lowness of our practice.

The point to which we aspire is near. We have not far to rise or far to fall. We live within small dimensions; we are seldom great either in virtue or transgression; we live too much in self, and while we do, we must live poorly. We cannot live greatly, until we get out of this individual self. We easily exhaust it, and then we must plod round and round, again, and again, and again, — a weary and monotonous revolution in the wretched slavery of habit. Our mere sensations have no distant limits, and we quickly reach them. There is nothing boundless, but God's universe and God's nature; there is nothing deathless, but excellence, truth and beauty; and it is only when we live in these, that we live in the measure and the majesty of our souls. Within scope more confined, we are fettered and imprisoned; and if the scope be our miserable self, it is as narrow as it is dark. We must be as a captive, who should vary the dreariness of his nights by counting the links of his chain, and amuse the tedious hours of his day by scratching his own portrait on the bare walls of his dungeons.

Christ is willing to be of us, but we do not permit it; he would be near us, but we place him at a distance, and this uncordial alienation we mistake for reverence. Christ consecrated human life; he exhibited its importance, and the more we are assimilated in spirit to Christ, the more this will be our sentiment. We cannot measure the results of *our* lives by *his*, for this indeed would be presumption; and yet, of the humblest life, it would be difficult to exaggerate the consequences. Our present life, in every turn of it, is leaving impressions on others that may enter radically into their moral existence, and not into theirs only, but through them, into many beyond any power of estimate. Blessed are we, if these are right; and woe unto us, if they are evil. And if unconsciously our life is thus influential, proportionately to the greater intensity is it so when we have a direct knowledge. Every thought willingly contemplated, every word meaningly spoken, every action freely done, consolidates itself in the character, and will project itself onward in a permanent continuity. The circumstances which at first we can rule, afterwards rule us. That which at first we choose, afterwards compels, and its sovereignty is not the less complete, that we do not feel it and we do not recognise it.

This law of existence is for encouragement and for fear. The man who fights bravely against temptation, has a consolation in knowing that he will pass from strife not only to ease, but to victory; the man who feels many requirements of duty to be hard self-denial, will find, with perseverance, this self-denial changed into self-enjoyment. In the opposite direction, the law is equally inevitable. No man gets rid of evil in the moment which bounds its actual continuance. It will infuse itself into the heart of thought, and again and again it will appear unbidden. That which once was hesitant will be spontaneous; passions will act without notice; desires will prompt without excitement; words spoken will seem of themselves to speak; and deeds done in times past with repugnance, will reproduce themselves apparently without agency and without volition. Here, then, are consequences the most momentous, and these are enfolded in our present existence. Here are consequences which concern our soul, and our soul's most essential interests, — the interests of its power, of freedom, of its dignity, of its peace.

The present life, therefore, involves consequences which stretch onward through progressive existence, consequences which are invested not alone with the importance of the world which now is, but the awfulness of that which is to come. To suppose that our existence should be continued in another stage of being, but that we should carry with us no whit of the character formed in this, is to me a supposition which I can reconcile with no possible mental or moral analogy. According to my apprehension, the supposition involves an entire oblivion of this world's experience, or a complete separation of one state of existence from the other; in different words, a loss of personal identity, and such is practically a loss of immortality. But if character is continuous, death does not obliterate its essence; that is within us now, it will be within us beyond the grave. Every present hour, therefore, is portion of an influence which will enter into our mysterious and illimitable consciousness; every present hour, therefore, partakes in the worth of an eternal intelligence; and this worth belongs to it, whether we esteem retribution temporary or everlasting, if we believe it to be in the character and in the soul. The idea which I have here endeavored to develope, of our present life, has all the grandeur which belongs to our undying nature; and only in this idea, I conceive, shall we measure it with a right appreciation.

Some words of practical inference are now all that remain to be said.

1. We should worthily comprehend our life. We should realize it in its grandeur and its completeness. We should feel that its most godlike attributes are not qualities which are to be an addition to its future state, but that they are a part of its very essence, and therefore belong to it in every moment. We should feel equally that what seem the humbler attributes of our life are no dishonor to its greatness, but in their due subordination, contribute to its perfection. Life cannot be mainly in pleasure, and the effort to make it so is resistance to nature and to heaven. But pleasure, notwithstanding, is a true element of life, and the austerity which would banish gaiety is not the religion which loves God as a Father, but the fear which crouches to him as a task-master. Let age have its grave discourse; but give youth its gladsome mirth and its griefless laughter. Whatever is pure in literature, graceful in art, beautiful in nature, cheerful in intercourse, let us all have as duty or opportunity permits; and while we do not abuse God's blessings, let us thankfully enjoy them. Life is not entirely in work; at least not in that work, in which so much of it is spent. We do not gain a fair compensation for our life in wealth or in worldly distinctions; and the life has been wasted, which has

been solely devoted to these, though a man could point to thrones which his ambition had won, or to millions which his diligence had gathered. To realize our true life, we must be conscious of the soul; we must know that life which is not supported by bread alone, which cannot be satisfied by pleasure, nor find its chief end in riches; that life which has affinity with all that tends to God, and grows by every word that proceeds out of his mouth.

2. We should be true to the relations of life. We should be true to its physical relations. The laws of health are the laws of God, as well as the laws of virtue; indeed, in many instances, the laws of health are the laws of virtue. It is needless to say how much usefulness may be lost by loss of health. When work is to be done, it is action and not intention that can do it; but how pure soever may be our intention, without strength, we cannot add our action. Nor is it the body alone that becomes feeble, but frequently the spirit suffers also; peevish tempers, irritable sensibilities, morbid desires, conspire to destroy its tranquillity; its amiability breaks down with want of peace, and those who love us are made unhappy, by sympathy with our pain, or by grief at our unreasonableness. Health is an essential of activity, and it is also a perennial source of cheerfulness; the objects around us have

their true appearances, the world and life, the things which it contains are perceived in their true dimensions; we are more inclined to be happy; we are more disposed to render others happy; we are better able to act, and we are better able to bear. To neglect, therefore, even this relation of our existence is a more solemn evil, than we usually esteem it. We should be true to the moral and spiritual relations of life, — its relations to heaven and to men; in spirit, in word, in action, maintaining purity, truth, mercy, justice, and beneficence. But upon such topics I need not here enlarge, as it is the whole business of the pulpit to explain and to enforce them. I would merely say, that our Creator has so inseparably united all the elements of our life, that we cannot fully gain its lowest good, and be indifferent to its highest nature; false to it in relations of the soul, it becomes all through gross, mean, impoverished, and we lose it even in matters of the senses.

Some few remarks of another kind, and I close. Persons may not be slaves to this world, because they are not always talking of another world. The deep mysteries of our higher existence, and the inward hopes and fears that belong to it, are too awful to be lightly syllabled. The experience which bears the soul beyond the confines of the flesh, which takes it from the lower arena of conflict to the upper sanctuary of peace, which leads it into communion with things not seen, and into converse with things not utterable; this is no subject for the common ear or for the passing hour. What is called religious conversation is often the least religious, often presumptuous, egotistical, impatient, disputatious, ungentle, and uncharitable. On the other hand, speech in which religion is not named, is frequently profoundly religious, replete with thoughtful sanctity, with gracious and elevated feeling, humble, courteous, merciful, and liberal; not wearying the ear with a round of phrases, but stirring the soul in its divine faculties, and acting on it with a transforming inspiration. Where such an inspiration is, it will not lose its power, even though it should not have an utterance. When Moses came down from the mountain, it was not by words the people knew that he had been with God, but by the glory that rested on his face. And so it is with all that live purely, and that live greatly. The brightness that comes with them from retirement, shows that they have been near to heaven. And persons may have their faces towards heaven, and their hearts too, and yet not be always thinking of it. That with which we have deepest sympathy is not forever present to our thoughts, and much less excitingly present. Extreme agitation robs us of that peace out of which there comes forth strength, — strength clad in the glorious panoply of God.

In the natural life, we are not better prepared, but worse for the coming stage, by propelling the mind too eagerly into it. The child hopes to be a boy, but does not torment himself in the interval with cares that have not come; and, the more he is really a child, the more he is unconscious, joyful, gleeful, happy, the more vigorous and proportioned will be his boyhood. The boy hopes to be a man, but in not dwelling with too intent anticipation on his manhood, but by meeting fully the conditions of his boyhood, by being all that a boy should be, he will be all the nobler man. Not unlike to the natural life is the spiritual life. Its healthy growth is continuous, and not by starts; in a regular succession, and not in impulsive efforts. When we try then, with all our minds, to comprehend our life, when we endeavor with all our hearts to be true to it, then let us patiently wait, gratefully accept, or faithfully submit, according to whatever Providence may order. What the hour that now is, honestly requires, that let us honestly be, and the next hour when it comes, will not find us unprepared. Always in harmony with the occasion, be it work or play, be it study or devotion, we may be at ease about the future, and go tranquilly along in the safety of a righteous conscience. Bearing bravely the evils that beset us, doing cheerfully the duties that are near, trusting in God, guided by Christ, fear shall not confound us in the way, and Death shall find us ready; then, as children following the messenger of a Parent, we shall pass into that unseen world to which Death is the solemn and mysterious herald.

"Know'st thou *yesterday*, its aim and reason?
Work'st thou well *to-day* for worthy things?
Then calmly wait the *morrow's* hidden season,
And fear not thou what hap soe'er it brings!"

THE PERSONALITY OF LIFE.

1 Cor. ii. 11.

FOR WHAT MAN KNOWETH THE THINGS OF A MAN, SAVE THE SPIRIT OF A MAN WHICH IS IN HIM?

The consciousness of another is impenetrable. We cannot reach it; we cannot even conceive of it. But in our own is our existence; our existence and our personality are the same; and, therefore, we shrink from the extinction of our personality, because it implies the extinction of our existence. Christianity teaches, in a variety of ways, the doctrine of a strict spiritual personality. Sometimes it connects this doctrine with the essential inwardness of a man's life; sometimes with the essential inwardness of a man's conscience; sometimes in warning, with the account he must render to his Maker; sometimes in rebuke, with the account that he would take of his brother. It is not the least remarkable characteristic of Christianity, that being of all religions the most social, it is likewise, of all religions, the most individualizing; that, of all religions, it is the only one which separates self-experience from self-indulgence; that unites self-sacrifice with self-regard; that brings meditation and action, comprehensive goodness and introspective thought, into full agreement. We shall look at this Christian doctrine, concerning the Personality of Life, in a variety of aspects. The spirit of the doctrine we take from the gospel; illustrations of it we shall seek for every where.

If we look into life, in itself, as each of us finds it in his own experience, as each of us finds it circumscribed in his individual consciousness, we become aware of a principle in our being, by which we are separate from the universe, and separate from one another. We become aware, that, by the power of this principle, we draw all the influences which act on us into our personality, and that, only as thus infused, do they constitute any portion of our inward life. It is by the power of this principle, which is, properly, myself, modifying all that is *not* myself, that I live, and that my life is independently my own. But some say, that man has no inherent spirituality, no spontaneous energy, no sovereign capacity. Such say, that man is never the master, but always the creature of circumstances. These are assertions to which no logic can be applied, and if a man, on consulting his own soul, is not convinced of their falsehood, there is no other method of conviction. No matter what may appear to be the external slavery, the external necessity of our condition, we still feel that we have a principle, an individuality of life, that is separate from our circumstances and above them. Take this feeling once away, and we are no longer rational, and we are no longer persons. And to this end, the utmost of human power is as feeble as an invisible atom. Human power may indeed so alter a man's condition as to alter his experience; to give him pain for pleasure, or pleasure for pain; to impoverish or to enrich him; to shake his heart with fear, or to entrance it with delight; but in every change his individuality is perfect and his own.

We do not, certainly, deny the influence of circumstances. In a great degree, circumstances are the materials out of which the life is made; and the quality of the materials must, of course, influence more or less the character of the life. But the connection of circumstances with life, the influence of circumstances on life, do not loosen the inviolability of its interior consciousness. This doctrine of circumstances affords no aid even for the interpretation of that in life, which may be interpreted; because, for a true interpretation, you should know all the circumstances that acted on the life, and you should know in what manner they acted. But who knows this of any one? Who knows it of one with whom he has been longest and nearest? Who can know it? Who can know the things of a man, save the spirit of a man which is in him? Race, country, era, creed, institutions, family, education, social station, employment, friend, companions, — these are but vague data when a soul is to be judged; and, be it only a judgment on the merest externals of character, such data afford, even for this, but uncertain inference. Perhaps things of which no one takes heed are the most important. A word heard in childhood, a kind or cruel look felt in youth, a tune, a picture, a prospect, a short visit, an accident, a casual acquaintance, a book, ay, the page of a book, — something, it may be, that observer's eye had never seen; something, that sank ineradically into memory, and never passed the lips, — these, and a thousand like, may be the chief constituents of many an impulse that begins a destiny. We behold the streams of individual life as they bubble out upon the surface, but we do not see the fountains whence they spring; we observe the fruit, sweet or bitter, which hangs upon the branches, but the roots are concealed from which it grows.

Every life has combinations of experience, of which another has not an idea, or the means of forming an idea. Every life has treasures of which others know not, out of which, and often when least expected, it can bring things new and old. But, did we know, and most exactly know, all the circumstances that enter into another's life, in what way they mingle with that life, in what way they become a part of it, it would still present to us an impenetrable mystery. How it is that events, incidents, objects, turns, and changes, alike in outward semblance, enter into millions of minds, and in every one of them assimilate with a different individuality. How one man is a poet, where another man is a sot; how one man is in raptures, where another is asleep; how one man is improved, where another is corrupted; how one man devotes himself to all that makes devotion great, where another finds nothing to attract him, but that which should repel him. Thus, whatever the visible appearances, within them, there is a central self, in which the essence of the man abides. Your life is yours, it is not mine. My life is mine, and not another's. It is not alone specific, it is individual. Human faculties are common, but that which converge these faculties into my identity, separates me from every other man. That other man cannot think my thoughts, he cannot speak my words, he cannot do my works. He cannot have my sins, I cannot have his virtues. I am as incapable of taking his place, as he is of taking mine. Each must feel, therefore, that his life must be his own. It has a training, and an impulse, and a power, and a purpose, which give him an independent personality ; and in the unfolding of that personality, consist the destiny of his life and its uses.

Life is first unfolded through outward nature. In that rudest state of humanity, which seems almost instinctive, we might imagine individuality as nearly impossible, but so it is not ; and monotonous as the ideas and experience may appear, they become incorporated with a distinct life, in the personality of each soul. But, does not outward nature afford manifest evidence, that it intended to unfold life through higher feelings than sensation ; sensation of that kind, I mean, which is merely necessary to animate existence ? Is there not other purpose for sight than discernment of our position and our way ? Is there not other purpose for hearing, than the simple perception of sound ? Why are there flowers in the field ? Why are blossoms on the trees ? Why in summer is such bloom upon the woods ; and why is autumn so clad with glory ? Why is the rainbow painted with hues so inimitable ? Why, indeed, is every natural object so shaped and colored, that the very sun seems but as a great light kindled in the midst of immensity, to illuminate and display the riches of its beauty ? Or, why, also, do the waves make music with the shore? Why do the airs make music in the groves? These are not necessary to feed, or lodge, or clothe us; they are not necessary to mere labor or mere intercourse. Did God lavish out this infinite wealth of adornment, which ministers nothing to bare bodily wants, which is not needed for bodily subsistence, not even for bodily comfort, that it should be as idle gaud and empty song in his inanimate creation, but afford no nutriment to the inherent life of his rational creatures? This cannot be, since we know, that the most imperfect life has a sense of beauty, and that in some lives it has the depth of an inspiration and the force of passion.

The life is indeed but narrowly unfolded, in which the sense of beauty in outward nature is dull or wanting. To walk over this goodly earth through the changing path of threescore years and ten; to take no note of time but by the almanac; not to mark the seasons, except by the profit or the loss they bring; to think of days and nights as mere alternations of toil and sleep; to discern in the river only its adaptation for factories; to associate the ocean only with facilities of traffic; to care not for the solemn revolutions of the earth through its circle in the stars; to have no eye for the infinity of sight; no hearing for the endless succession of sounds, — sights and sounds, that vary ever as the earth rolls on; to be blind, and deaf, and callous, to all but the hardest uses of creation, — is to leave out of conscious being whatever gives the universe its most vital reality. Such a life may be called a prudent life, and, for its object, it may be an eminently successful life; but its object is paltry, and its success on the level of its object. Not that men are expected to be poets or artists, or to have the peculiar temperaments that characterize poets or artists. Not that men are expected to talk of their experience of enjoyment in nature, or to affect it, if they have it not. The ready exposure of any intimate emotion is unmanly as well as ungraceful. When true, it is offensive; when false, it is disgusting. The pretence of emotion is among the vilest of hypocrisies; the cant of sensibility is one of the worst depravities of language. Not that men are expected to relax in the rugged duties of private or public industry, which are equally necessary and honorable; not that they are expected to spend weeks, or even days in the woods and fields, or watch the courses of the stars, indolently to meditate and moralize; I merely insist that the sensibilities be open to every influence of natural beauty; I speak of the life that is strictly personal, and I hold that such life is greatly enriched which gathers as much of these as it can into its experience. If these sensibilities belong not to the individual constitution, there is a deficit in it. If the world has deadened them, the world has done the being a serious injury; if educational or religious culture has not been such as to incite them, each has failed in one of the most vital offices of a true spiritual culture. For it is not in mere sensibility alone to beauty, that life is unfolded by means of outward nature. Outward nature, also, unfolds life by exercising thought; not thought which is busied only about wants, but thought which delights to seek the end of creation's laws and mysteries. But life is unfolded in its loftiest capacities, when every where in outward nature the soul is conscious of God's pervading presence; when it sees the goodness of God in all that is lovely, and the wisdom of God in all that is true. "A thing of beauty it has been seeing, is a joy forever." But it is not a joy at all, until it becomes mingled with a human life. A child wanders by a stream. The stream would babble onward, whether the child were there or not; but when the child mingles his laughter with its babbling, it is then a thing of beauty and a thing of joy. Every man, whether he knows it or not, is an incarnation of the immortal; and through his immortality all things that connect themselves with his soul are immortal. In every loving soul, therefore, according to the measure and exent of its power, God re-constructs the heavens and the earth.

The individual being of man is also unfolded by society. It is born into society, and by society it lives. Existing at first in passive and unconscious instincts, it finds protection in the care of intelligent affections. The home, therefore, is the first circle within which personality opens, and it is always the nearest. Beyond this, the individual is surrounded with circumstances more complex. He is cast among persons whose wills are not only different from his own, but constantly antagonistic to it. And thus in society, as in nature, the unfolding of his being will be by resistance as well as by affinity. The most self-complete personality can have no development but by means of society ; and the more it has largeness of capacity, the more it has fullness of thought, the more it has greatness of feeling, the more it has aptitude for action, the more it needs society ; the more it needs society to draw out its faculties and to engage them. Intellect works by means of society. Thinkers the most abstract have not all their materials of reflection in themselves. The studies that belong purely to the mind as well as those that belong to matter, and to the active relations of life, require observation, comparison, sagacity, variety of acquisition, and experience. No man can be a thinker by mere self-contemplation. He might as well expect to become a physiognomist by always gazing in a mirror, or to become a geographer by measuring the dimensions of his chamber. A man is revealed even to himself by the action on him of external things, and of other minds. According to the measure of the sphere in which a man is placed, and his sufficiency to fill it; according to the force of the influences which operate upon him, and his ability to give them form and direction, must be the expansion of his being. Society is, of consequence, a necessity, not to the growth merely of thought, but to its very existence. The body could as easily breathe without an atmosphere, as the mind could cogitate without society.

Thinkers, the most abstract as well as the most practical, have been men of the world, and men in it. Aristotle was a courtier; so was Lord Bacon; and no modern politician is more among crowds, than was the mighty-minded Socrates. Imagination works by means of society. For society it builds and sculptures, paints, — forms its concords of sweet sounds, and puts its dreams into melody and measure. Of the men who have done these things so supremely, as to gain immortal names, many were reared in cities, and nearly all labored in them. Among such we may especially name the great poets, and, as not the least remarkable, the bards of rural life. In contrast with crowded places and artificial objects, men felt with quick delight the influences of God's uncontaminated creation, while many whose dwellings were embosomed in the secluded peace of nature, slept through life and into death without awaking to any knowledge or enjoyment of their inheritance.

But for society, virtue could neither have existence nor a name. Society, and society alone, by its obligations and injunctions, by the contact in which it places will to will, by its excitements and its sympathies, elicits the power of the moral nature: society it is, that trains this power, tries it, strengthens, matures it; is the arena of its contest, is the field of its victories. But if in society the moral nature has its contests, in society also it has its charities. There are the blind, the deaf, the feeble, the disordered body, and the disordered mind; there are the widow, and the orphan, and the forlorn aged; there are the poverty-stricken, with thoughts bewildered in the puzzling meditations of distress; parents that look mournfully on their children, and children that gaze bewildered on their parents; there are the ignorant, the guilty, and the enslaved. In society, there is, indeed, abundant tribulation, but in the heart of man there is abundant mercy, a fountain of goodness, exhaustless and sublime. The religious sentiment works by means of society. The simplest possible idea of religion, is an idea of relations; for without the sense of dependence, of duty, and of devotion, we cannot even conceive of religion. Christianity represents these relations always by images the most intimately social; in God, it teaches us to find a Father; in man, a brother; in the church, a household, a communion, a household of faith, a communion of saints. But the passions work also by means of society; and their depravity and dominion are but too sadly apparent in the strifes and corruption, which are bounded only by the power of our nature, and by the limits of our race. Too surely are they manifested in the envy, hatred, malice, and all uncharitableness, which poison and disturb communities; tremendously are they felt, when, in their compacted vastness, they gather to the blackness of a fury that eclipses the light above us, and into hurricanes of wrath that shake the world.

But while society, whether in calm or conflict, unfolds life, to this its agency should be bounded. It should not be allowed to absorb the individual life, or to crush it. With the strength, the freedom, the integrity of thought and conscience; with honest and unoffending idiosyncrasies, it has no claim to interfere. When this interference threatens, or invades any serious right of a man's personality, at any sacrifice but the sacrifice of duty, the personality must be vindicated. The natural power of society, or combinations in society, will always be as strong as they are insidious; and let a man guard his independence as vigilantly as he can, when watched the most jealously, it will never be too secure. Men in our age live gregariously; and if the aggregation were for exertion and for work, this might be a benefit; but men think, men feel conventionally, and this is an evil. It enfeebles, it impoverishes the life, it depresses, nay, it denounces originality, it takes away all stimulus to meditation, reflection, or any strong mental effort. I deny not that we owe a decent respect to the consent of numbers in thought and action; and let it have all the respect which it can fairly claim. The sanction of time, also, may deserve our veneration; nor should we ever treat such a sanction with levity. I do not impeach the value of public opinion, and I cannot but admit its power. But I do not bow to it as an authority, nor accept it as a guide.

Life in our age is too much in the mass for any thorough spiritual culture; and life is too much in the outward for any intensity of individual character. Men are looking beyond, when they should look within themselves; they are anxious for the good of the community, when they should be at work to mould their own nature to the best conformation of which it is susceptible. If those who use efforts for others, and use them seriously, would first use them to the utmost on their own spirits, society would advance more quickly towards regeneration. Just as one supreme work has a more elevating influence upon art, than thousands that are imperfect, so one really complete and harmonious character does more to raise the community than scores which fail of power and proportion. Society unfolds the life to a true end, only when it respects, while aiming to improve the individual, his inward, his really inalienable rights. It may correct, it may chastise, I will not say that it may kill, — but these it has no title to outrage. The individual has the authority, and, if he will, he has the power, to resist such usurpation, to hold his inner being as his own, and to preserve inviolable its individuality and independence. Let every man do this, and for the same reason that he respects his own personality, let him respect that of every other. Let every man, I say, hold his personality sacred: let him do so, because he will thus build a nobler virtue for himself; because he will thus exercise a juster influence on his neighbor, and because the combinations which grow out of sympathies free and independent, have that real union, wherein is strength. Let not even the consciousness of having done evil, break down the strength of this personality.

There is a mawkish tendency in some, to charge their failings on this or that cause out of themselves. They were tempted, the evil was placed in their way, and they could neither pass by it nor bound over it. This is a dastard, craven, cowardly spirit; a base, mean, cringing spirit, which, after all, absolves not from the transgression, while it pulls down the soul into the deepest pit of degradation. It is just as far from genuine repentance and humility, as it is from honesty and heroism. If any one has done wrong, let him manfully admit it; let him, as he ought, charge it on himself, and take the penalty; let him not accept of escape, which would be the perfection of disgrace by stripping him of his moral manhood; let him not evade his personal responsibility, and thus cast away the last fragment of honor that may remain with humanity even after guilt. Those who in the least aid a man in this degrading self-deception; who weaken, however slightly, the solemn monitions that belong only to strictly personal conviction, — commit a fatal error; for this is the proper basis of social as well as individual morals. Shake this, and nothing is secure. When we judge others, we must make every merciful allowance; but we must not teach themselves to do so; nor must we do so when we judge ourselves.

I have said that we should hold every man's personality sacred, as well as our own,—and I repeat it. Why should I wish to compel any man, if such were possible, to live my life, think my thoughts, accept my opinions, believe my creed, worship at my altar, devote himself to my views, and enrol himself in my party? If such desire were not utterly foolish, would it not be the climax of presumption? But to be cold towards him, to avoid him, or be angry because he will not, this is something worse than folly or presumption,—it is the malevolence of a bigot. Some one may object, that the personality which I defend is an obstinate egotism. Not at all. Nor is it combative or exacting, but charitable and liberal. The absence of a true individuality produces many of the gloomiest evils with which society is deformed. Why else do people consider the meat as more than the life, and the raiment more than the body? Why else do they so esteem that which is not their being, and so little that which is? Why else do they so sicken for fine houses, and gay clothes, and great feasts, and the chief places in the resorts of fashion? Why, also, do they so fiercely envy those who have them? Why else do people ape the talents of others, and neglect those which are their own? Why do they so abortively attempt the work they cannot do, and overlook the work they can? The want of individuality gives force to all the imitative and all the emulating passions, out of which silent or outward strife proceeds.

Let a man be satisfied to be himself, and he will not be dissatisfied because he is not another. He will not, then, be hostile to that other for being what he is; nay, he will rejoice in all by which that other is ennobled; he will lament for all by which he is degraded. For a man, therefore, to be himself, fully, honestly, completely, does not circumscribe his communion, — it makes it wider. But a man should not be content to be only roughly himself. A man ought to labor to beautify and harmonize in his interior personality; and if that be done, there will be no confusion in his exterior relationships. And what a glorious work is this! If the sculptor spends years in toil to shape hard marble into grace, and then dies contented, what should not a man be willing to bear and do, when it is a deathless spirit that he forms to immortal loveliness? Gratify inclination, speak as the blood prompts, act as selfish volition or selfish desires command, and all will be disorder. A man must not allow this. He must test his nature by external facts; he must find its relations to general laws; he must accept these laws reverently and obediently. Still, the work of training must mainly be his own, and it must consist with the inviolable personality of spiritual, individual, immortal existence.

After all, there is much of one's life that is not unfolded; much that remains uncommunicated, or that is incommunicable. The very medium, language, by which spirit holds converse with spirit, is inadequate to transmit the plainest thought as it is in the mind of the speaker. Language is not representative, but suggestive, and no merely spiritual idea is exactly the same in any two minds. No word therefore can be, to any two minds, the sign of an import that absolutely corresponds in both. How much of life passes within us, that we make no attempt to impart, that we have no opportunity to impart. Nor is this so only with those whose lot is isolated; it is so with all, — with the most social, with those whose homes are full, and who spend large portions of their time in domestic and general society. The man who has the most intimate circle, and has it constantly about him, leads a life that is greatly more in solitude than in company. How much of our life passes in our walks, in our journeyings, in our labors, in our rest, and all in the depths of unbroken silence. The man who has spoken huge volumes, the man who has written such, has yet given out but a mere fraction of his existence. The whole of no human being's life is known to another, possessed by another, though that other be in the closest and most constant communion with the life.

If we find such to be our ordinary experience in life, what shall we say of its more solemn passages? Can any man, and let him be of surpassing eloquence, communicate an absorbing thought, and the interest with which it fills him? Can any man cause another to burn with the rapture in which his soul exults in certain moments, when excited by a scene of beauty? No: we try in vain to express an overflowing joy, as vainly do we attempt to put into utterance a deeply-seated grief. What words will translate the beatings of a youthful mother's heart, when she looks into the face of her first-born? What language has man yet spoken, which can make fit confession of the deadly and the dread remorse which a duellist, not dehumanized, must endure, with every recollection of his victim? Even bodily pain, we cannot make the most sympathizing understand; and when the visitation of sickness lays us low, when the head is burning, and the heart is faint, and the eye is dim, though tenderest ministries be around the pillow, we are alone, we have emotions which we cannot, if we would, impart. And then Death—Death always in shadow, always in silence, always absolute in isolation!

Who, then, can know the things of a man, save the spirit of a man which is in him? What misgivings, what memories, what darkening fears, what dawning hopes, may then agitate the breast, and none can know, and none can share them! Our friends may weep, they may call on us, they may warm us with their kisses, they may bathe us with their tears, but the spirit is shut in, and its earthly communion is over. What is that with which the spirit of the tyrant, of the oppressor, of the hard-hearted, of him who bought gold by iniquity, of him who climbed to power through slaughter, — what is that with which such spirits are shut in? What vision opens upon expiring Dives? What brightens the closing eye of dying Lazarus? We shall not seek to pierce the mystery. These solemn isolations, we ought not to forget; they must, sooner or later, come to us all, and it is but common prudence to gather strength to meet them.

I have spoken mostly of that in all men which they cannot speak; which, if they could, none would understand; but more inscrutable still are the great ones of our race. They walk among men as mysteries and alone. How companionless in spirit must the men always have been, who were far before their age, in wisdom or in goodness. The sage comes with his thought, and his generation mocks it; a century or centuries must pass, before it begins to be a fact. The seer comes with his warning, and those whom he would deliver, stone and kill him. The apostle with his doctrines, and the philanthropist with his plans; they must wait until Time gives at once the exposition and the confirmation. But in the heart of Jesus, above all, what mysteries and worlds there must have been of unshared and incommunicable sanctity and goodness! What a life was his, so isolated, so unshared: what a life in such an age; but if man could not comprehend it, it was comprehended of God; and belonging, as it did, to Eternity, it was impossible for the passing day to know it.

The view that I have given in this discourse of life, some, I doubt not, will consider lonely. I have not spoken but with full persuasion of the fact; and I have done my best to give a clear statement of it, with its arguments and illustrations. A great part of life must indeed be lonely, and that is often not the worst part. In a pure and reflective loneliness there is strength, and there is depth in it. There is great enrichment in it. To get at the meanings and mysteries of things, we must converse with them alone. Every man, therefore, in whom the highest life finds expression, must in many ways be a lonely man. So the thinker is lonely; the poet is lonely; the hero is lonely; the saint is lonely; the martyr is lonely. Social affection has, indeed, great beauty; public spirit much worth; energetic talents have abundant utility; but it is by habits of independent and solitary meditation, that they are matured, deepened, and consolidated. In this way a man enlarges his life, while he individualizes it; every sphere of being then lives in him and he in that, so that his individuality has no limit, but the limits of its faculties, and the limits of their exercise.

Yet, if much that I have spoken on man's personality, on the inwardness and the incommunicableness that belong to his deepest and most real life, may be questioned, two positions I will refer to, on one of which our present experience can decide; the other lies for trial in that great Future which the veil of flesh conceals. The one is, that in which a man feels placed for judgment before his secret self; and still more, if he acknowledges and is conscious of it, — God's Holy Presence. But let it be only himself, and even then, poor and fallible as conscience may be, his sin will find him; the wrong that he has caused or done, the misery he has occasioned or inflicted, will often come to him in memories charged with terror; though he should be in the midst of ten thousand, they will come to him alone; though he could grasp in thought the whole population of the world, he will be conscious that on him only the charge is made, that he only in this case is the being meant, that he only is the being guilty. Here, at least, is a strict, individual personality; and though a man may blind himself to the witness of God, God has so ordered it, that he cannot entirely be blind to the witness in himself. And in that other, hidden behind the grave, where man cannot by easy speeches and fair looks, appear to be what he is not; while most revealed, he will be most individualized. When illusions are over, when the distractions of sense, the vagaries of fancy, and the tumults of passion have dissolved even before the body is cold, which once they so thronged and agitated, the soul merges into intellect, intellect into conscience, conscience into the unbroken, awful solitude of its own personal accountability; and though the inhabitants of the universe were within the spirit's ken, this personal accountability is as strictly alone and unshared, as if no being were throughout immensity but the spirit and its God. The word written in the sacred book, declares that "every one of us shall give account of himself to God," and this is but a transcript of an earlier word, of "the law written in the heart."

THE CONTINUITY OF LIFE.

JOSHUA X. 12.

SUN, STAND THOU STILL UPON GIBEON; AND THOU, MOON, IN THE VALLEY OF AJALON!

SUN, stand thou still! How often is this the prayer of the heart! O why, think some, should rising and setting suns bear me so rapidly out of my youth! so soon take away my pleasures! so soon take away my beauty and my strength! Why do days so pass into weeks, and weeks into years, and years, not creep but fly, until we tremble as we count them! Why is time so inexorably rapid, and so cruel in his rapidity! Why take bloom from the cheek, and buoyancy from the step! Why so freeze the blood, and why so bleach the hair! O sun, stand thou still, and let not my life, and all that is fresh and ardent about my life, and in it, be carried off before I have enjoyed them, — almost before I have felt them!

O sun, stand thou still, desires another, that I may "pull down my barns and build greater; that I may have wherein to bestow my fruits and my goods; that I may say to my soul, Soul, thou hast much goods laid up for many years to come; take thine ease, eat, drink, and be merry." O sun, stand thou still, lengthen out the day of toil, that my hirelings and my slaves may work the longer, and that I may grow rich the more abundantly!

How contrary the prayer would be with others. Not, sun, stand thou still; but, O sun, hasten on thy way! hasten on, O sun, and bring me tidings from the absent! hasten on, O sun, and bring me the expected triumph! hasten on, O sun, and let the day of revelry appear! be not so slow and lingering in thy course; weary me not with waiting, but speed me to the hour for which my soul so yearns! Hasten on, O sun! Let the time be quick, which is to glorify my name and crown my ambition; which is to crush my enemies and to exalt myself.

Hasten on, O sun! exclaims another. Let me have the quiet and consoling night; let my tortured eye have its shadow, and my burning head its coolness. Hasten back, O sun! cries such a one again; bring to my watching sight the beauty of thy morning beams. Chase away this killing darkness, which weighs down my spirit with its dismal heaviness; wake up the heavens, cheer the earth, bring to my fainting heart the music and the hope of a new day.

Hasten on, O sun! sighs the prisoner. Hasten on, O sun! so quicken thy pace, that days may be hours, and hours be shortened into minutes! Hasten on, O sun, that the term of my captivity be fulfilled; that I may once again walk unfettered among men; that I may tread the green pastures, and breathe the untainted air.

Sun, stand thou still! murmurs the sentenced criminal, whose last sun is shining. O sun, stand thou still, and give me some more of life! Let this heart pant yet longer; let this warm blood flow on! keep off the moment which brings with it the sound of death! O move not, as thou art moving, with rapidity thus terrible! do not quicken the pendulum, but retard it! prolong the intervals which are the measures of thy speed, and check those deadly vibrations that echo mortality in every beat!

But not for wishes, prayers, not for enjoyment or despair, does the sun stand still or hasten onward. Bright, serene, but inexorable, the sun moves onward through immeasurable space, with his group of planets around him; ours, with its myriads of animated beings among them, — at once the cradle and the grave of associated life and death. The planet turns upon its axis, and revolves about the sun; but suns greater than ours, with their systems, travel onward and ever through the realms of space. The hosts of worlds, by their vastness, are beyond all compass of locality and time; they are only to be comprehended within immensity and eternity. These views are given us by the sages and the teachers of science; and they are written for our learning, for lessons of wisdom, and lessons of humility. *We* are involved in this universal, unceasing, continuous, resistless motion. We are encompassed by it, in our material relations, subject to it; and our life, in these relations, and all that depends on them, stands no moment still.

Life to opening consciousness is a novelty, and full of wonder. Curiosity is the philosophy of childhood; and most quick, most diligent, and most honest is its teaching. Interest attaches to every thing around childhood, and so every thing fastens its attention. The child does not analyze, but enjoy; and, life not logic, is the general principle in the child's mental experience. The child puts his own life into whatever he perceives, so that all being to him is animate, and thus he feels with it; and in his own way converses thus with nature. Sun, moon, stars, trees, flowers, live to him. In this sense the child is a poet, and the poet is a child. The poet is the everlasting child; but he is more, — he is likewise the everlasting man; and he is therefore the most exalted poet, in whose genius there is most of innocence and most of wisdom.

But, unlike the poet, the child's existence is all in the present; it is an existence which has neither past nor future. It is in the senses, in the first wants of animal being, in affections few, kindred, and instinctive. But as intellect begins to think, as fancy gathers analogies and images; as fancy and intellect act upon sensations; as memory stores the mind with incidents, and adds firmness to readiness of impression; existence becomes enlarged, it is raised out of the present, it catches glimpses of the distant, and it looks into the future. But this future is all of this world, and this world seems to youth immortal.

The future of youth is deathless and endless; and though it beholds age failing under the weight of years; though it may have wept scalding tears in the house of mourning, and sobbed on the margin of the fresh-made grave, — they are facts with which it cannot connect itself in any intimate sense of reality. Though this era of life is transient as any other, it has a kind of mental permanence, from its endearment to memory, and its attractiveness to imagination. And in a true, natural, unperverted childhood and youth; a childhood and youth that have had fair justice done to their spontaneous qualities, there is much to render them thus endearing and attractive. The things that belong to such a childhood, such a youth, are indeed sweet and lovely. The illusions that belong to it are beautiful; the dim mystery around the studded canopy of the skies; the desire to touch the horizon on the mountain's brow; the necromancies of night; the voices of spirits; the romances of Fairy land; the tales of Araby; the love of light, and gaiety, and flowers; the enjoyment of action; the transmission of its own feelings to surrounding objects: sympathies with the life of nature; untaught inquiries into the profundities of existence,—these are all, not of common, but even of sublime interest; and not the elements of poetry only, but the germs also of philosophy. The affections that belong to such a childhood, such a youth, are pure: the love of kindred; the joy of confidence; the disinterested kindness; the unstained tears of pity; the unsuspecting charities which spring up in the soul, yet unspoiled by contact with the world; the frank and generous friendship, which pretension or hypocrisy has never yet corroded; the depth and struggle of undefined sensation; the cheerfulness and the fervor, that cause the face of heaven to shine more brightly, and the stream of joy to flow more copious and more sparkling, and the pulse to beat stronger in the bosom, and the blood to rush warmer in the veins. The disappointments, which originate so many evil dispositions in after-life, are yet hidden from youth. The lottery of life, yet undrawn, has not given the lie to expectation; experience has not worn out pleasure, nor laid bare the fallacies of hope; emulation has not yet commenced the hard strife of worldliness; as yet success provokes not the hatred of jealousy, nor is failure darkened by the envy of despair.

How natural, then, that we should cling to whatever is associated with our childhood and our youth. Youth is so pleasant, that it is hard ever to think it gone,— utterly, absolutely, and forever *gone*. Nay, we would fain believe it yet remaining, in spite of wrinkles and white hairs!—An old age of virtue has many and noble compensations; the experience that well-used years have left; the repose that honest toil has earned; the reverence that merit commands; the willing homage that is paid to wisdom;—but to youth, only, belong the excitements of impulse, and the mystic charms of pursuit. As our sun climbs to the meridian, we think not of its setting; as it passes the meridian, we are not zealous to reckon its degrees; when it is almost below the horizon, we turn back, and wistfully we gaze upon its reflected image in the sky. If we ever had things good or happy in our lives, the thought of our youth recalls them, and it recalls them with all the poetry that belongs to the Past of individual experience. It awakens memories of the most sacred relations, of the freshest affections, of the noblest friendships, of the deepest hopes, of the most generous aims; and though disappointment or satiety, or guilt or sorrow, may since have intervened, yet such memories and meditations have an influence for good, even if their beauty should be pallid with sadness.

It is probable, however, that in one period of life memory dwells upon the past with as much of illusion, as in another hope looked onward to the future. Childhood and youth, even when not unblessed, have their sorrows and their sins, mental anguish and moral pain, — pain often amounting to remorse; and though they may not tell such feelings, or indeed know how to tell them, it is not less certain that they have them. I am fully persuaded, without the shadow of a doubt, that children often endure a keenness of misery, of which we form no conception; and I am also persuaded, that if we reflected more on the inward history of our own own early years, we should do more justice to the feelings of childhood. Look, therefore, on childhood thoughtfully and pitifully. Cloud not any of its innocent delights; and because even childhood is human, it must have sorrow, but add not to its sorrow; because even childhood is human, it cannot have unmingled bliss, rob it of no bliss that nature allows it. Look upon childhood gently and reverently.

Being, in childhood, it is true, is limited; limited in its dimensions, senses, affections, passions, — but it is embosomed in the infinite, and among its first ideas is that of the boundless. We awaken into life with a vague sense of its grandeur. We fancy that we can reach the sky which rests upon the mountain, but the weariness with which we pass through the measure of a few fields, tells us in what a big world we are living. The stars seem near, and we think that we could grasp them, but soon we begin to suspect the vastness of the lighted dome, and then there dawn upon our faculties glimpses of the measureless universe of God. O wonderful period, when, within the little brain and bosom, there lie enfolded the germs of all thought, all action, all passion, all genius, and power, and dominion; of virtue and of guilt, of glory and of shame, of rapture and despair. When you behold a child gladsome in the sun, look not on through the gloom of your own worldly knowledge, but rather try to catch some brightness from its unsuspecting joy. Let it have the joy itself can make; leave it by the streamlet; let it roll among the flowers; let it chase, but not kill the butterfly; let it prance and run in the ecstasy of motion; let it prattle, as if unheard, its own invented tragedies and comedies.

If it smile, give it your kindest look; if it weep, kiss away its tears; if it be weary, take it to your bosom, lay the hand of blessing on its head, whisper the word of peace to its heart, put a simple prayer upon its lips, — but never, never awaken its fears or rebuke its hopes, or chill its exuberance, by casting over it the influence of your own seared, faded, discontented, worn-out experience.

But soon that youth, which once appeared as endless, is, distinctively, no more, and we find ourselves engaged in the actions and interests of the world, with such strength of faculty and purpose as we have. Then begins the real history of life. Behold the stirrings of civilized men, — how wide, how deep, how multifarious, and how sustained. Go to the courses of travel, and crowds are there; go to the places of commerce, and crowds are there; go to the courts of law, and crowds are there; go to the camps of armies, and crowds are there; go to the legislatures of nations, and crowds are there; go to the abodes of wealth, and crowds are there; go to the receptacles of indigence, and greater crowds are there; go to the houses of feasting, and crowds are there; go to the houses of mourning, and the *solitary* are there. But, further, behold what these crowds have done, and are doing. They have changed the desert into a fruitful field;

they have built these cities; they have adorned and enriched them; every structure, desirable and grand, is the creation of their strength. They have formed the roads that intersect the land; they have made and manned the fleets that traverse the sea; whatever proclaims the dominion of power, skill, labor, art, and all combined, they have accomplished. They have completed wonders which astonish us; they will prepare for wonders which will astonish others. To limit our inspection of these things merely to the outside would leave but a very inadequate impression. Going below the visible, we see in them marvellous results of thought, patience, industry, force, passion, genius. We see in them, also, things that must have been occasions of the strongest excitements, and things that link themselves still with much of strife and selfishness. Feelings, however, of the good and true are not absent. These are the things of man's maturity; and every honest and active man has his part in the life, of which they are the outward signs.

But though men *work*, in a great measure, collectively, they do not *live* collectively; the deeper life is in the breast or in the home, — and this, especially, is woman's life. Within the breast are the passions, — some that spend their force in the world, and some that exhaust themselves within; some that will not reveal themselves, and some that cannot. Within the breast and within the home are the affections, with their most exacting cares, and their most rewarding pleasures; and out of the noises of the world, or in those hours when such noises are subdued, we will not believe that earth is poor in the number of the breasts and the homes, — whose affections, whose thoughts, true to their cares, abound in their reward. Gain what triumphs a man may, — fortune in business, applause among nations, favor with rulers, love among the people, a name to last in literature, admiration in the senate, glory in the field, — if his inward and his near life is bad or barren, he is unhappy; and though the splendor of his circumstances may conceal the malady of his spirit, it cannot cure it.

I have not mentioned the moral and religious feelings, because they should not mark any distinct stage of life, but be in the whole of it a continuous and unbroken inspiration. But the passions, labors, and the affections, if they do not find their end with the end of maturity, they begin their strength with the beginning of it. We speak, of course, with no strict accuracy; for though we may note an era of life, when its characteristics became manifest, we have no faculty so keen as to discover, infallibly, its commencement or its conclusion. But, rudely considered, we seem in our maturity for a while to stand; we look before and after; in the opening, life is all in the future; in the close, life is all in the past; but in maturity, the future and the past appear to divide it equally between them; experience sobers hope,—but hope, there is yet enough to brighten memory.

A few years roll forward, — and hope there must be to cross the boundary of Time, or the memory of life, instead of being to us the dawn, the morning of immortality, is but an atomic spark in the boundless gloom of nothingness. I speak thus of life under no prompting of an uncheerful spirit. Throughout these remarks I have kept in view a full and complete earthly life; full in the largest measure of its years; complete in all the faculties of body and of mind; complete in all the relations of a social and civilized humanity. If we take earth and time as the measure of human existence, a life thus ordered is all but perfect. It is then to the age of such that I refer; not to the age of one defiled with early vices; not to the age of one broken with afflictions, overclouded with disappointments; not to the age of one made solitary by strokes of death, silent and successive, that cut down associates as they became friends, and children as they became companions; not to the age of a life so confused by reverses, failures, and mistakes, as to seem not only aimless, but anomalous; no, — not to such do I refer, but to the hale and healthy age of a vigorous, and, in the worldly sense, a successful life.

Youth is of the future — maturity, of the future and the past — childhood has nothing but the present — and age, nothing but the past. But to an age even as felicitous as that which I have described, we can scarcely conceive the position to be cheering, which has nothing in one direction but the past, and nothing in the other but a blank. *The present*, no old age can be properly said to have, — at least, the sensitive and energetic present. New sensations, fresh impulses, quick alternations of desire, rapid motions, intense passions, plans, projects, enterprises, are not for the dim eye, the deaf ear, the rigid nerve, the sluggish blood, and the conservative habits of intellect and opinion, which both the mental and physical influence of age tend to consolidate. The tendency in age to look back is inevitable; this also weakens the consciousness of the present. But, if nothing else had such result, the apparent rapidity of time to age would have it.

Have I stated a paradox? It may be; but I have stated a truth, which I fear not to be tested. Explained it might be on abstract principles, but ours is no right occasion for metaphysics. The fact before us needs no confirmation, but that which a reference to simple experience can afford. We feel, all of us, that as Time slackens the machinery of life within us, it flies past us with accelerated speed. It is marked, not by motion in the soul, but by shadows on the dial. The afternoon has come: we are conscious of little but of the lengthening of the shadow. All we know is, that the evening has approached, and that the line which it has reached indicates the nearness of sunset.

The true life of age is spiritual; and the life which it has lived, if it can be turned to any value, must be subjected to a spiritual transmutation. To make the idea plainer, let us take a brief retrospect of the course we have pursued, and place before us, in one unbroken view, the succession and continuity of life. Curiosity and sensation, as we have noticed, are the distinctive elements of childhood; susceptibility is the leading one of youth; strength, passion, feeling, *will*, all that constitutes *character*, belong to maturity; reflectiveness is the prominent attribute of age.

Now what, according to this order, would be the distinguishing condition of each stage, supposing that a right culture be joined with nature? We will not go into particulars; but how should we broadly designate each period, — conceive each as it ought to be? Should we not specify childhood as the period of spontaneousness, — that of youth, the period of discipline,— that of maturity, the period of action, — that of age, the period of tranquillity? In childhood we should look for simplicity, — in youth for teachableness, — in maturity for diligence, — in age for wisdom. The affections proper for each we should look for in each, modified *in* each by the moral form and tendency incident to its development; in childhood by trustfulness; in youth by generosity; in maturity by devotedness, and the spirit of sacrifice; in age by tenderness, and the calmness of wisdom; and while we would not exclude age from hilarity and enthusiasm, we would not absolve youth from self-denial and self-culture. And these are bound one to another by the law of sequence; and, if not interpreted too literally and strictly, we should say in the order of cause and effect.

We should seek for the issue of a spontaneous childhood in the discipline of youth; and for the issue of an instructed youth in the action of maturity; and for the issues of an active maturity in the tranquillity of age. It were delusion to suppose that Memory should not often appear, as an accusing angel, to disturb this tranquillity, and that conscience should not admit the accusation; but memory we should also expect to be often to it an angel of light, in whom the voice of the past was a message of good-will. It were delusion to suppose that this tranquillity must not be shaken by many painful agitations; but we would trust that they would not reach its centre, — firm and steadfast in a faith and hope which secured it against every vicissitude of time.

Conceive life otherwise, — and we may not simply conceive it, — we can see it and we can feel it. Conceive much in each portion of life to be ineptitude or misuse. If childhood is lost, or to the degree it is lost, youth is injured; and so to the end, in the measure of the preceding neglect or evil. Youth can never do what childhood has left undone; and maturity can never act for youth. Whatever we have allowed to pass, we have allowed to perish. Childhood, youth, maturity, — when they once have gone, are no more ours to re-construct, than the empires of Rome, Persia, and Assyria. The last hour is as much out of our reach, as the centuries that lie between us and the flood, — the last year, as the ages that lie beyond it.

We can imagine what is yet worse, — the order of life, not confused, but reversed. Childhood, instead of being spontaneous and trustful, may by poverty, with the presence of vice before it, become cunning, reflective, suspicious, and deceitful; youth may have no training, but bad training; maturity may be but the hardihood of selfishness; and age may not be wise, but foolish, — not tranquil, but garrulous; it may be the slave of vanities that rob gray hairs of honor, — or of a worldliness, that shuts out goodness from the soul, and fills it with unworthy care. To feel that the past is irrecoverable is melancholy enough; but the idea of an irremediable present is an idea of despair. We shall not dwell upon it. To think that, at the best, only amendment is possible with us, not restoration, is in itself an impressively solemn thought.

With Time there is no propitiation; nothing that you can give will stand with Time, instead of using it. To be sure, as you can change from a good life to a bad one, at any point, so you may indeed change from a bad life to a good one; but though you lose the past in the one case, you do not gain it in the other. Time is vindictive and irreconcilable. Time accepts no sacrifice; it admits of neither redemption nor atonement. *It is the true avenger.* Your enemy may become your friend, — your injurer may do you justice, — but Time is inexorable, and has no mercy.

I am tempted here to make a general application of this truth. How often, in homes, do the ruling minds lose sight of the inevitable law of continuity under which those are growing, with the care of whose existence they are charged. Upon a wider sphere we can observe a similar disregard. Nations have their youth as well as individuals; and they may abuse their youth as well as individuals; then, as surely, they will reap the fruits of the abuse, in an unprincipled career, and in premature decay. Rulers commit a great wrong against a people, and a people commit a great wrong against themselves, whenever they put expediency for right, and whenever they estimate success alone as glory. The future will disappoint expectation in all that the present, in such instances, may promise it. Whatever may come of temporary profit to immediate generations, for millions there is prepared an inheritance of trouble. Sow but one seed of primal evil in the moral soil of a nation, it will grow to be a tree as broad as the sky, — to take fruitfulness from the earth wherein it is rooted, and to cover it instead with barrenness and gloom. And there it will stand fast, until it falls by its own corruption, or until it is torn up by the fiat of divine judgment, or by the hurricane of human passion.

The individual application, however, is to us the most important. "In all the actions which a man performs," says Owen Feltham, "some part of his life passes. We die while doing that for which our sliding life was granted. Nay, though we do nothing, Time keeps his constant pace, and flies as fast in idleness as in employment. Whether we play or labor, or sleep, or dance, or study, the sun posts on, and the sand runs. An hour of vice is as long as an hour of virtue. But, the difference between good and bad actions is infinite. Good actions, though they diminish our time here as well as bad actions, yet they lay up for us a happiness in eternity, and will recompense what they take away by a plentiful return at last." Wise words are these and good; wise and good they are, for they are true; and, because wise and good and true, worthy of attention and acceptance. Yet the outward continuity and change which make that which we call Time, has deepest import from the inward continuity and change, with which they keep a constant and steady pace.

Time is the exponent of life, but life has its continuity and changes in the soul, and not in the continuity and changes of the circling earth around the sun. No fact of emotion or of action stands alone; none is bound to the duration of its *felt* existence; each is linked to each, and all constitute the oneness of an inseparable identity. Within us, is that law of continuity, which connects one part of life with another, and without which there would be no wholeness of life. The law of continuity which thus connects the inward life itself, connects it likewise with the universe, and with the Infinite Mind, which is the life of the universe. This inward continuity is the spiritual chain of life, — and the feelings, the thuoghts, the desires, the memories, the habits, which it binds or holds together, are strong to lift us up to peace, or to pull us down to misery.

However the inward life may be, it is the changes of the outward that mark its course. Look, I pray you, on the blithesome boy who lingers and loiters on his way to school; who thus lingers and loiters, because the vitality that throbs within him shrinks from the most temporary suppression; look at the same being in the lean and slippered pantaloon, when he loiters and lingers near the grave, and how startling, how impressive is the contrast. Yet, are they but too points in the progression of the same life, and which feels that it is the same life. Look at the young girl, with the glow of summer's dawn upon her cheek; with the brightness of heaven's sun, the depth of its star-light in her eyes; with the gladness of innocent maidenhood in her breast; or the lights and shadows, the ecstasies and sorrows of approaching womanhood flitting athwart her beating heart, in visions of dreamy, undefined, but most impassioned prophecies; look at her as she trips across the field with a step so gay that it scarcely bends the flower; look at her as she glides through the mazes of the dance, so measured, so graceful, but yet so vital; so calm in countenance, so profound in feeling, so simple in manner, so fathomless in enthusiasm, so little comprehended by superficial gazers, and such a mystery even to herself! Look at her once again in the decline of age, and here again we have extremes inseparably united, but, outwardly, in stern contrast.

And thus does life go on, until Death accomplishes the catastrophe in silence, takes the worn frame within his hand, and, as if it were a dried-up scroll, crumbles it in his grasp to ashes. The monuments of kingdoms, too, shall disappear. Still the globe shall move; still the stars shall burn; still the sun shall paint its colors on the day, and its colors on the year. What, then, is the individual, or what even is the race in the sublime reckonings of Time? Years, centuries, cycles, are nothing to these. The sun that measures out the ages of our planet is not a second-hand on the great dial of the universe.

There is, however, that in our race, which Time, in its most tremendous movements, cannot exhaust; the continuity of life, sympathy, conscience, reason, which live along forever; the magnetic links which interpret the heart of man to man throughout the line of ages. This continuity transcends all force, and is independent of all time. Supremely, continuity exists in the immortality of the individual, in the immortality of the race. Neither are right and truth seared by time; indeed, they alone escape; these we can hold, without change and without accident. Other things we can no more retain, than we can stop that motion which gives a night to every day, and a winter to every year. We watch the retiring light; we linger on the clouds it purples; we close our eyes to muse, and when we open them again, the darkness is about us. Our ambitions and our vanities wither before us like the gourds of a night, and we, as the prophet, lean over them and weep.

But in such sorrow there is no strength, and for such, no consolation. Bloom will depart from the field, and splendor from the grove; the seed-time will come, and the harvest pass away; and on *us* too, if our year of life continues, winter will fall. We cannot, for our wish or for our bidding, expect the sun to stand still, nor the moon to stop her course; fruitless would be our word, however vehement our desire; though we should cry out with the collected supplication of mankind, "O sun, stand thou still upon Gibeon; and thou, moon, in the valley of Ajalon!" There is no Gibeon in life, upon which we can rest for a moment, the morning or the noon-tide; there is no Ajalon in age, whereon we can force the moonlight to repose beyond its appointed hour. We cannot rekindle the morning beams of childhood; we cannot recall the noontide glory of youth; we cannot bring back the perfect day of maturity; we cannot fix the evening rays of age, in the shadowy horizon; but we can cherish that goodness which is the sweetness of childhood, the joy of youth, the strength of maturity, the honor of old age, and the bliss of saints.

THE STRUGGLE OF LIFE.

EPH. vi. 12.

WE WRESTLE NOT AGAINST FLESH AND BLOOD, BUT AGAINST PRINCIPALITIES, AGAINST POWERS.

MAN combines in himself in the highest measure that we know of limited existence, sensation and activity. By sensation, he is a part of nature, by activity he is out of nature and above it. By sensation, he is subject to nature; but by activity, nature is subject to him. By sensation, he sinks into the general mass of unthinking being; by activity, in the degree of its force, elevation and rectitude, he becomes emancipated from this mass, and lives in the likeness of God. Between these two tendencies, the life of man is by necessity a struggle; a struggle in which the life is truest as the higher element prevails, and the lower one but serves for the unfolding of the higher. And this it does, as we perceive, when we trace it in the tendencies of the species. Consider man in his meanest estate, — he is then the most defenceless of creatures. Nature has given him no weapons, nor even instincts of protection, and of all creatures he is the most in danger. He is exposed to strong and furious beasts, and, different from all other animals, he is also exposed to those of his own kind. Sensation leaves him helpless; it is activity, — that is, mind, reason, reflection, will, — that gives him power. He gains sovereignty over beasts, and forms associations of kindred and counsel with beings of his own species; thence all governments. His naked hand cannot meet the multiplicity of his wants, and so he seeks out many inventions; thence all the arts.

But man reflects on what he does; out of reflection comes the method of doing it; method elicits plan, plan principles, and thence all sciences. Thus, as art is at first the contrivance of thought born of necessity, science is the thought separated from the contrivance, and expanded by reflection. Out of this again come further inventions and greater arts. As man is at first a thinker by the wants of sense, he is afterwards a thinker by the wants of mind. The same law which governs his doing and his thinking, governs also his utterance; for both the wants of sense and thought, he must have a medium of receiving and of imparting knowledge; thence language, and ultimately all literatures. Within this brief view, we have the cause of struggle in man's life, and the true direction of it.

The cause consists in man's dependence upon nature by sensation, united with his capacity by activity to rise above nature and to rule it. The true direction is towards a more free and a more expanded being.

Let us view this struggle in relation merely to life in its earthly arrangements.

In the primitive state of life, the urgency of want leads to action — to action which is directed to meet the urgency. If the want gets no farther than sensation, the primitive state hardens into a savage state. If the want become progressive, so will the urgency — and so will the activity. The life advances. In states far removed from the primitive in what we call civilization, the struggle of life with the wants of mere sensation, has more tendency to oppress and to degrade than to impel or to improve. In the primitive state, man soon discovers that he has no artificial provision to depend on, and so he puts himself into rude and earnest strife with nature. He sees his destiny immediately, and at once he girds himself to meet it. In doing this, he puts forth his strength, and feels his power. He battles for his life, but he lives in the consciousness of victory. In the civilized state, the struggle with the wants of mere sensation is very different. Nature is shut out by a thousand barriers. Sea, forest, river are owned; beast, bird, and fish are banished or guarded. The strife is not then with nature, but with artificialism; not with brutes and elements, but with men or circumstances; not in freedom, but in subjection. The consciousness of strength is not here, but that of weakness, and life is not the prize of combat, but the wages of servitude. Pressed on these lower wants, life in civilization, depends on servitude or cunning, and oftentimes on both; with sufferings and sins of both, it becomes involved in melancholy complication. The child enters the world without provision and without welcome, and, when it begins to understand life, it has its earliest cogitations in the perplexing problem of how hunger is to be allayed, with no visible means of procuring food. The first attempts at solving this problem, involved and knotty as it becomes in old society, are to many the beginnings of a life that thickens with crime and misfortune to the close, and there is lost in darkness.

It would be wrong to say that the struggle in civilization with such wants is always attended with debasement. On the contrary, it is, in cases numberless, maintained with a heroism and patience that show how great man can be in lowliness, and how rich with nothing but his enduring soul. I speak only of tendencies, yet of tendencies, however, which are based upon facts, not deduced from analogies. Multitudes, and without blame, are engaged in it with a perpetual enlistment: in the worst states of society many rise above it; and in the best some fall down to it. With the ordinary provisions of civilized society, the more difficult struggle is with ease and facility. The struggle is, to choose labor and self-coercion, when the present seems to offer indolence and pleasure. This is the temptation of our youth, and to overcome it, is to enter on experience with the advantage of an opening conquest.

While life is young, if inclination could have its way, we would spend it all in sport and motion. The discipline of school, the counsel of elders, the restraint of parents, clashing as they do with the promptings of our blood, if not accepted in faith, must, of necessity, be most cheerless and disagreeable. Yet, when that faith gives us victory over desire, and tramples down repugnance, we attain to calm and bright spots, from which, as we look back, we can perceive how true, and safe, and wise, and loving, the guidance was, by which we were directed. And we perceive also, how dismal, perplexed, and dark our lot might have been, had we, instead of resisting passion, resisted duty. The resistance, it is true, cost us pain. We gave ourselves to solitude and study, that, without obedience, would have been hateful drudgery. We denied ourselves the sunny field and the shady wood, when our hearts leaped against our bosoms to enjoy them. To be right was in itself sufficient, but rectitude had its hope and its recompense of reward. Lessons ceased to be tasks, and in time they became knowledge; knowledge made us useful, and with years, it may be, made us wise. To all, lawful sacrifice and work have their due return. Comfort and independence abide with those who can postpone their desires, and wait while the fruit ripens which their toil has planted. Can you find any man who has applied or is applying his toil to the best advantage, and who has reaped or is reaping the most fruit from it, — be it competence, wealth, political eminence, professional success, scholarly reputation, — that has not gained his position by numerous victories over opposing solicitations. Even he whom the world calls inspired, does not put forth his inspiration with no cost of struggle.

To say that genius needs no labor, is as absurd as to say it can be obtained by labor. Both errors are alike exploded. But a capacity for great labor belongs to eminent genius, and is necessary to it. When we look at the works which some men of even short lives have left, — to say nothing on the toil of mind, on the extent of studies, on the vastness of knowledge, on the multifarious arts and acquisitions which such works imply, — we are confounded at the fatigue of hand alone which must have been borne in simply transcribing them. We know, moreover, that the authors of not a few of them were feeble or afflicted men, — men who composed them often amidst the distractions of adversity, or under physical or mental suffering. But if men will not struggle while they may, they will have to struggle afterwards, — when they must. The boy may devote himself to play, and permit no check upon his instincts; but with resulting ignorance, he will often have to encounter sordid hardships and oppressive labor, from which education might have saved him. The youth may give himself to ease, while he can find support provided for him; but when that fails, as fail it must with many, he will then have to struggle with habits of idleness; or he will have to struggle with want, which idleness must entail; or he will have to struggle with the insults which dependent indolence must endure; and besides all, he must struggle with his own goaded spirit, until it is scourged, tamed, utterly broken down to the abject contentment that befits his slavery. Even the man of genius, who fails to close his eyes and ears when the syren of gaiety smiles and sings; who twines the bay with the rose and the vine-leaf, and steeps the garland in the wine-cup; who prefers the luxury of musing to the labor of meditation, will have to bear the humiliation of a waning fame; while others that have been more faithful, are rising with a light upon the world which grows brighter and brighter towards the perfect day.

Let us view this struggle in relation to life in its spiritual and everlasting interests.

Man meets resistance in the outward world and in his senses to material and mental effort, but through this very resistance, he puts forth his effort and goes on to power. But the obstacles to his moral and spiritual advancement are most within himself. With these are, indeed, the great struggles of life. Let us say nothing of these tendencies which show themselves in external masses of ruin, that defy all attempts to discriminate or analyze them. And yet, mighty as they seem, the individual soul is not lost in them. Thick and overwhelming as the clouds of transgression are which hang over our earth, every drop in them has been distilled out of a human heart, and had relation to a human history. Now of all the millions of these histories, each had its peculiarities, each had its own struggles, its own trials, its own measure of culpability, and its own share of retribution. How few even of the worst were not conscious of a fall; how many of them wrestled with their convictions, hard and long it may be; how many of them, also, withstood their temptations; but not one of them escaped the disorder which moral derangement brings upon the spirit, and the gloom which it casts upon experience of the life. Wantonly and indifferent many may appear, openly regardless of all that is of worth, reckless of whatever is most sacred; but the inward life and secret hours have anguish that is not seen, and which should not, if it could, be told.

I have to deal with matters which do not thus show themselves, — struggles that, if more subtle, are often not less fatal. It is not needed for me to dwell on distinct cases, which, to the rudest, the most blunted conscience, are acknowledged sin. At such points, the struggle is commonly at an end, either in confirmed victory, or confirmed apathy. There are things that grow on us by little and little, which do not provoke contest, and seem at first scarcely to deserve it, — that, like many despised enemies, become at last formidable. Temper, for instance. This appears, first, in simple petulance, and, while connected with youth and with affection, is only in manner a pleasant individual exhibition of wilfulness. But see it as it becomes incrusted into habit; as years grow, observe it harden into obstinacy, or otherwise, as it may be, unfold itself in unappeasable discontent and irritation.

The miseries which are caused in life by unamiable temper alone, if one could see them in the mass, or conceive them in detail, would terrify and chill him.

How harmless, also, does vanity appear in its ordinary guise, and no malignity is deeper than that which it can engender. Under fair address, under refined appearances, in company with smooth phrases, it can condense into a hatred that is, in its silence, more deadly than the fierceness of armies in their shock. Imperceptible, too, is the growth of selfishness. Every sin may be resolved into selfishness: but here I mean the selfishness that has direct application to one's own personal feeling and objects. Slowly and insidiously it creeps upon us, and, before we are aware, it has possession of our nature. By following an insect up a rock, a soldier found a way into a fortress, that had been demed unapproachable and impregnable ; and there is no passion, if it go upon the trail of our selfishness, but can enter the citadel of the soul ; and the passion which gets in by such an entrance, it will be ever the hardest to expel.

Under these influences, sins may be committed, the guilt of which we may not fully discern, until many days and years have gone, — sins of unkindness, — sins of envy, — sins of personal desire, — sins of which we may repent, but never can forget, — sins which we might weep for till the fountains of our tears were dry, but which would still be burning as ever in their memories of remorse, — sins that will often haunt us in faces of sorrow, that afflict us the more bitterly because they look on us with no anger. If these did us no other harm, they interfere with the direction of our thoughts, they break down the strength of our faculties, and they disturb the unity of our purpose. These, or any other violations of charity or justice, of affection or of conscience, must be met by instant and complete resistance, if we would have true or independent lives. No one that heeds experience will make little of slight neglects. They have the seeds in them of increase; they will grow and multiply, and become as moral cankers in the soul. The finest sensibility may decay, and if not joined to effort, and upheld by genuine activity, it will die.

It is in the tendencies, least marked and least visible in life, that we have the most to strive with; it is in the depths and retirements of the soul that the great battle must be fought; it is with resistant forces that come never to the surface. Much is said about the ruling passion. This saying presupposes that each individual, with any marked elements of character, has some distinct passion which governs him. The inference is drawn from observing some leading habit of his mind and of his life. This, then, according to such philosophy, is the tendency that he has the most to watch, to counteract, and to control. If the philosophy is at all sound in theory, it is very uncertain of application, and very difficult of practice. To be of any efficiency, the individual himself must have the knowledge, and he himself alone can to any purpose alone act on it. Thus the very centre of the remedy is likewise the centre of the disease, — or, more properly, the same individual is patient and doctor in his own case, and must be so; yet that which constitutes him patient, is the most likely to baffle and to blind him as doctor. For how is this predominant passion to be discovered, or when? Before it becomes predominant, it is not within the conditions of our question, and after it has become so it is beyond them. The fact of its ascendancy implies its strong dominion over him who is called on to guide it; and he who needs to be the most watchful of its lures, it is the nature of these lures to deceive.

It is a common assertion, that a man is not the best judge of his own talent. The remark may be extended to the moral nature, and add, — that a man is not the best judge of his own temptation. What outward notice decides to be a man's besetting evils, but few men will in the least acknowledge. In this state they are not separate actions, but fixed habits; and habits are, of course, unconscious. They are, moreover, generally such habits as are not scandalous, such as the world tolerates, — often associated with concomitants which the world either approves or flatters. The outside deception of life coincides with inside ignorance of the heart, and both unite to obscure the conscience. Besides, as respects this asserted ruling passion, some views of it are incomplete and others are false.

No single passion despotically rules any sane life. Every life in its course has many alternating passions, many conflicting and many mixed passions. Nor is there any object of a life, however constant and prevailing the object may be in acting on the direction of the life, that does not consist with a multitude of other interests and inclinations. Moreover, the passion which seems to rule the life, was not originally the deepest in the life, and is not the one which would have prevailed, if the will could have decided. The dominant habit, therefore, may be nothing more than a substitute for the strongest passion; a man may be in a counting-house, who longed to be in a camp, and who, as he cannot make war, turns with all his might to make money. A man may be in the camp, who would have been, had his inclination served him, in the cabinet, and who is amidst the toils of war, because he missed his aspirings in the ambition of peace. Thus do matters proceed in the world; to the on-looking eye, the semblance of one life; to the *infeeling* spirit, the consciousness of another. The truth is, the most potent desire of a man's nature, is the most open to disappointment; for the strength of his hope is rarely equal to the force of his appreciation, and the weakness of his hope communicates itself to his purpose. It is not, then, at a single point of life, or on a single spot, that we have to struggle, but all around it, and all within it.

Happy are those who do so with perseverance and success, and who find as they advance a brighter way and more confirmed power. Yet, so far I have not surveyed the whole of the struggle, and even were the victory so far secure, it would still be imperfect. Our life is not complete, even when in full harmony with Time and with our kind. There are feelings, sentiments, capacities, which go beyond these and above them. They are in us, and if comparison can be, they are not only the most real things in us, but they give to whatever also belongs to us — reality. Reflection on a spiritual life may be, to some, but as dreaming, as words spoken in sleep — words with no meaning and without coherency. Not many, however, are they who so think. The solemn ideas of Christianity; its estimate of the soul; the inwardness of its morality; its views of God, of Jesus, of life; of goodness; of immortality; the grandeur of its faith and hope; the compass of its charity; the awfulness, yet the consolations with which it invests the death-bed, the grave, the passage through them, and the sphere beyond, will often ask for entrance to the most careless minds, and if they do not gain it freely, they will by force.

There are no minds upon which questions of a higher life will not frequently press themselves ; and there are no minds that can shrink from them into complete indifference. A sense of the infinite and mysterious universe in which they are ; of the inscrutible being which they have, will often stir them at unexpected turns, and move them with vast anxieties ; the effects may be evanescent, but they prove the profoundness and power of the inner life. In this inner life, too, we have to struggle ; we have to struggle with the things that tend to deaden it or to keep it dormant ; with the senses, with the pains, that, by the senses, bind us only to the present. Even the best feelings and the most innocent enjoyments have their share in withdrawing the life from absolute and everlasting realities, or from hindering its apprehension of them.

It is hard for us, in contact always with palpable objects, feeling life mostly in this contact ; pressed by demands and needs that stop never for a moment ; actuated by motives that by necessity are near to us ; moved likewise by immediate pleasures and immediate pains ; it is hard, I say, for us, to bring home to ourselves, that aught besides has any substantial being.

And yet we have not penetrated into life, until we feel that these are not at all its substance, but only its circumstances. It is still harder, agitated as we are by such a variety of interests and desires, with their strength within and their objects at hand, to take as our law, as our only law, the dictates of invisible power, and the injunctions of a perfect, a passionless will. And yet, as that is the one which must prevail, not against that, but against our own is the wisdom of the struggle. That must rule the order of Being; out of the order, we have nothing but disappointments and humiliation; within it only, can we have capacity and freedom.

In connection with the spiritual life itself, we have trials, doubts, fears, distress of soul, seasons of great and exceeding trouble. Faith, trust, and humility, are the only strength with which we can encounter these trials; and then, with patience, we shall overcome, and have the reward in peace. Periods have been in the experience of some, when their faith was simple, when trust was childlike, when they rested meekly on the Everlasting Father; they have since lost that experience; they have plunged into a lower life, and left the higher one so far away, that what once was as spontaneous as their breathing, has become a perplexity or chimera. But they have not found satisfaction; they have only tasted of mocking luxury, of luxury such as that which comes to a hungry man in the visions of the night, that torments him in sleep, and disappear on his awaking. They have but wandered in twilight, or with changing and uncertain limitation ; they have discovered that what they esteemed greatness at a distance, became littleness as they approached, and shadow when they passed it. The thoughts of past experience bring back regret, but not belief — its image in the memory, but no renewal of it in the soul. Let such thoughts, however, be encouraged, for they may be the heralds of restoration and return.

But it may be inquired, shall the senses, the passions, the world, the ordinary occupations and enjoyments of men, be exterminated in this struggle for a more elevated existence? Shall victory rejoice amidst the wrecks of feeling and memory ; and the brow wear the laurel, only when the heart is hardened? By no means ; the struggle is not to destroy any part of life, but for the harmony of all its parts ; not for the disruption of life, but for its unity. The thing that we have to do with our inward life, is to bring its latent capacities and forces into exercise ; to acquire sovereignty in the control of them, and, from their action and their uses, derive constant accessions of energy and excellence. It is to apply the spiritual mind in the spiritual life, as we apply the practical mind in the common life ; it is to give us as grand a dominion in the region of ideas, senses, feelings, and passions, as we hold in the region of earth, air, and ocean. It is in the one as in the other — to make things that resist, obey us — to make things that oppose, subservient to us — to make obstacles yield to action, and become the occasions of further and future triumphs. This would be the science of the soul, the philosophy of the spirit, the wisdom of the conscience — a science, a philosophy, and a wisdom, as much surpassing all other science, philosophy and wisdom, as the everlasting does the temporary, as the changeless does the mutable.

To gain and grow in power, — power, which shall be vital, constant, continuous, — is to cultivate the spiritual part of our being; and this, not by paroxysms, but by habitual, simple, natural exercises of its proper faculties. Let faith, for instance, the desire for truth, the consciousness of God as all in all, the love of duty and the love of man — let these mingle with the workings of the soul, let them rather *be* its workings, then life may take its course. There is no need to discriminate between the activities of business and those of religion, for both in this high idea of life are one — they are the same. And this high idea of life, is but the idea of man's natural and right existence. In prayer or at the plough, in the workshop or in senates, such life has equal dignity — the only dignity that man can truly have — the dignity which consists in living in the order of his best nature, and in the use of his best faculties.

But spiritual action is only secure and perfect with practice. To minds of a certain temperament and constitution, elevation of thought, of feeling, and of devotion, may give way to very fatal errors of conduct. The excitements of religion, if not corrected by the soberness of meditation and by the diligence of charity, are not far from lower excitements, and often slide into them. Men cannot always, even in religion, live in raptures, and ecstasy may be as fatal as despair. The soul wears out by excess even sooner than the body, and turbulent emotions are the most ruinous of intoxications. It is hard to descend from these, and to find only common objects — daily routine, vulgar toil, and unideal duty. The fall below the ordinary life may then be as great as the exaltation was above it.

And thus we easily account for instances of startling moral contrasts in the same man, which the world insists on placing in the catalogue of hypocrisies. Though I die with thee, yet, will I not deny thee, exclaimed Peter to his Master. Even without divine knowledge this would have warned the Master of

Peter's infirmity. In this very ardor of a rash zeal, lay the weakness that did before an hour deny the Christ for whom he swore to die; and, as if to show to all men how true character is to itself, to whatever it may be false besides, he was as vehement in his apostasy as he was in his profession. Had Peter in his spirit been nearer to things as they were, he would not have vowed and asseverated, he would have been humble, he would have been silent, and he would have been faithful; collected in his strength, when the hour came, he would have been superior to its trial. But he was bold and over-confident; his enemies caught him unprepared, and shame and defeat befel him. By combining the fervor of religion with the activities of goodness, these dangers are counteracted. Nor this only, for by such a combination, the fervency of piety is changed into a divine usefulness. The motives, the doings, the endurance, of such consecrated excellence, which come not with observation, though as nothing in the workings of the world's noise, are of the kingdom of Heaven in the workings of the world's silence.

The highest life which we can have is contained in the practical life. The life which we now live, we live in the flesh, and that is the life which we have to struggle with and train, safest, as I have shown it is, when it is not one of mere sentiment and thought, however grand the thought, or however generous the sentiment. Ideas and feelings must, as I have already observed, be combined with moral discipline and benevolent action. And this is the life that is best for individuals, and best for society. Accept the being good, and the doing of good, as evidence of sanctity, then the communion of saints would be a large one, and though still there must be struggle in the soul, less of struggle would be among the churches. The communion founded on the doing of good is a broad one, and they who are united in it agree to leave many differences out of sight. They work in peace, they work together; and not *for* the work, but *in* the work, they have their exceeding great reward. And often this work must be done not in pleasure, but in suffering.

The path which leads to the mount of ascension does not lie among flowers; and he who travels it, must climb the cold hill-side, he must have his feet cut by the pointed rocks, he must faint in the dark valley, he must not seldom have his rest at midnight on the desert sand. It is no small thing for which a true liver strives. It is for the perfection, for the sanctification of humanity in himself and in the world. It is not by ease that this is to be done, but by efforts grand and blessed.

Uneasy, it has been written, is the head that wears a

crown; but the genuine man, every real Christian man, is a king; and he must meet responsibilities of a royalty more solemn than mere earthly monarchs know, or would care to accept. But, if rest is not to be had in the wearing of a crown, how far must it be from the carrying of a cross? Yet every Christian man must bear a cross — must be a martyr — must pass through the tribulation of his Calvary. But what a hallowed power is that which can calmly walk to it — which can silence the complainings of the spirit, and go forth bravely to the work of Heaven.

THE DISCIPLINE OF LIFE.

Job xii. 8.

SPEAK TO THE EARTH, AND IT WILL TEACH THEE.

Speak to the earth, and it will teach thee of God: it will teach thee in every blade of grass of his creative power — in every unfolding leaf of his creative wisdom — in day and night, in climate and season — in all living being, it will teach thee of his ever-providing goodness. Speak to the earth, and in the continuity of its revolution, it will teach thee of order; in the dissolution and renewal of all that it contains, it will teach thee of change. Look up from it to the silent heavens, and you learn of Eternity; look down to it on the withering flower, and you learn of Time, yet with an analogy infinitely inadequate. Speak to the earth, and it will teach thee of Man. It will teach thee that his visible existence, in its longest and its widest measures, is but fleeting. It bears but few evidences of its proudest races; all that remain of them are, here and there, a few lettered pages, and a few mouldered stones. The rest it has swallowed up, and of them it has preserved neither note nor name. Embosomed in immensity it rolls around the sun, and now the clash of Alexander's battles are no more to it, than the rattle that diverts a child, and the majesty of Cesar's fortunes as insignificant in its throng of interests as the story of a beggar's wants. It will teach thee, that, now, too, as ever, it continues to absorb the visible, that the pyramids shall crumble, that cities shall turn to fine dust, that men in time to come will look in vain for Paris or London, that wolves shall howl where monarchs feast, and that towered palaces shall arise where the wild flocks pasture. Speak to the earth, and it will teach thee, that these, too, will depart, and be replaced; and that, when eras shall have past away, and be to other eras as if they never were, the whole is not yet as a moment, even in the limited reckonings of Time. Speak to the earth, and it will teach thee, that the men who are now living around thee, who now constitute the busy population of the globe, — the wise, the great, the good, the rich, the beautiful, the famed, the admired — are daily and hourly falling into the abyss of atoms — as well as the ignorant, the lowly, the guilty, the poor, the homely, the obscure, the despised — and that not many suns shall have set, when all will be in the same oblivion together.

Speak to the earth, and it will teach thee of thyself. It will teach that thou art of these departing things, that every turn of it brings thee rapidly to be of the forgotten ones. Speak to the earth, it cannot teach thee more. It gives thee the lesson of humility; it does not give thee the lesson of hope, it abases thy pride; it does not awaken thy faith, it forbids presumption, it does not instruct for preparation. Speak to the earth, and it will not teach thee of the great plan which includes all things, and which has a place and a worth for the infant's rattle as well as Alexander's wars, a place for the beggar's story as well as for Cæsar's fortunes. It will not teach thee of the supreme Wisdom, by which that plan is conceived, directed, and accomplished. It will not teach thee of thine own relations to that plan, and how thou mayst best fulfill them. For this, consult a Teacher that has a voice, for earth to such desire is dumb; consult Christ, and he will teach thee truly; consult a Teacher that has a spirit; for earth to such yearnings is lifeless; consult conscience, and follow the promptings of its higher inspirations; consult thy mind in its full tranquillity, and respect the counsel which it gives; consult experience, when it is most likely to be impartial, and take heed to its honest warnings and rebukes.

Two kinds of agency enter into the discipline of life.

There are first the elements that constitute the matter of life itself. These elements are such as make the inward and outward history of the individual being. Among these, for instance, are our parentage, our early circumstances, our means of instruction or our unavoidable ignorance, our advantages for virtue or our exposure to vice, our examples for good or evil, our peculiar tendencies and temperaments. Most of these begin before we have ourselves any part of a voluntary nature in them, before we have any dominion over them. They, in general, continue long to operate, before we undertake in any way to shape or to guide them. In a multitude of cases, they meet with no guidance or control whatever, either from without or from within. In such cases, the result is speedily wrought out, and I need not say that the result is, uniformly, one of suffering or of sin. The matter which makes the history of life, continues always, however, to be also an influence of life. The course of our studies, the activity of our business, the nature of our opinions, the nature of our friendships, the force of our affections, our health and sickness, our success or failures, our poverty or wealth, or ideas of poverty and wealth, — all, in fact, that makes the sum of our being, physical, social, moral, and spiritual.

The second kind of agency is that which we exercise of ourselves, and upon ourselves. A man is thus both the object and the agent of his own discipline. This kind of discipline cannot be too early begun, it cannot be too late continued. It may be too long deferred, but, however advanced the hour, none at any time in the day of life should despair to commence it. It is by this agency of ourselves, that we turn all things to account, that we make them our true property. It is by this agency, that we draw all influences into the sphere of our inward life, and cause them to become, in part, the substance of that life. In proportion to the depth, the power, and the compass of this agency, are the depth, power, and the compass of our life. Without this agency, much passes around and near us, that might be used to enlarge and to glorify our being, goes wholly to waste, and to us is forever lost. Many an influence that we allow to die, we might convert into living energy, and many a good that is present, and at no cost, but the taking of it, we lose because we never perceive it. And this is not all the loss. But that which belongs essentially to ourselves, which forms the very vitality of our souls, fails of its growth, its strength, and its complete capacity. Memories pass away in dreams, that might have been turned to fine principles, and resolves perish into vacancy, that, if executed, might have been noble works. Designs are left to sink into nothingness, that, if brought out to the light of reality, might avert occurrences that will be pangs to the hour of death, or be benefits to many, and blessings to ourselves. Intellectual and spiritual advancement is thus prevented, the mind given over to barrenness, and the character not enriched, seems even worse and poorer than it is, either in motive or in fact. The agency that we exercise upon ourselves, is the one to which I more particularly refer in these remarks on the discipline of life.

But what, we may ask, is this discipline to act on? To this we may oppose another question, What is any education to act on, but, on the human being, on the soul and its manifestations, on thought, on feeling, on habit, on conduct?

It requires some discipline to *think*, in the true sense, at all. We might suppose that nothing was so easy as to *think*. What is it? It requires not to move hand or foot, but to sit still and ponder. It appears as if it needed but to let the brain work, and let memory observe and register the result. Certainly, ever, and ever without ceasing, perceptions are passing through the brain, and consciousness is without interruption, taking impressions from the senses, — but to arrange and concentrate these so as to extract an import from them for judgment and the reason, this is the hardest task that man can undertake, and it is the one of all others that he would avoid. He would, in general, dig or break stones rather than to do it.

It is thus, that whenever a real thought is born, it first meets with resistance, but, when accepted, soon becomes a tradition. It then settles as a fixed point, becomes the centre of a sect or party. While friends are whirling around this, they imagine their motion progressive, when it is merely circular, and when they fancy themselves numberless degrees on a direct line, they have not extended their distance by the smallest measure. Thought merely in itself being an exercise, that we most sedulously shun, that we would by any means escape or evade, it must be no common effort to think constantly, to think wisely, to think vigilantly, to think on matters which hold out no immediate profit or reward, things not palpable, and things not seen. If thought on our most ordinary affairs is painful, and what, if we could, we would not undergo, it is not to be expected, that we should enter willingly on thought which concerns mainly the order of our spiritual and moral being. It is not then in the least startling, that our lives should be full of mistakes, of errors, of prejudices, of unexamined generalities, which we count for knowledge, and of ignorance, which time only serves to render darker and more obstinate. For a man to *think* boldly around himself and within, is no small courage, and it is only an occasionally brave and strong soul that attempts it. It is a hard and self-denying toil. To test our opinions by their external evidence or their intrinsic value; to separate them from influences that, independently of their value or their evidence, bind us strongly to them; to review our beliefs and motives; to estimate, without sophistry or illusion, the consequences of our doings; to go through all this, fully and fairly, would seem little short of a mental martyrdom. And yet the habit of a true moral wisdom is to be thus obtained.

Now we know, that feeling not under the guidance of thought is but blind impulse, and habits growing out of such impulse, even if blameless, become only mechanical routine. Conduct formed of feelings and habits thus shaped and moved, can at best be merely negative. But, though guilt should not be in the life, life may, notwithstanding, suffer positive and serious injury. I will remark only on the influence of feeling. How many of the woes of life arise from undisciplined feeling. How many thus rush into careers, positions, and relations for which they are not fitted, and wear out their minds, or become disgusted with existence. How many, too impatient to wait for experience, rushed on their path through an illusive sunshine, and while, still dazzled with the gilded sky beyond, met destruction over the unnoted precipice.

To speak at large on the regulation or disorder of feeling, would be to speak volumes. Take one error of it, which is mostly an error of the young, and that is, the hasty bestowal of confidence. It would be delightful to live in perfect trust, to doubt no one, and to believe all. The spontaneous action of the soul is that alone in which there is true joy, and it seems a hard and a sad requirement, that any thing should meet it with impediment or revulsion. Were our nature in perfect order, we might trust entirely to our intentions and our impulses, and with others, likewise, we might trust their intentions and impulses. Words we might take as copies of thoughts, promises as the utterance of intentions, the clasp of the hand as the pressure of friendship, and the smile upon the face as the sunshine of the heart; and this is what noble, ingenuous, earnest, simple youth does.

I would not lessen this trusting temper of youth, I would only warn it; I would not have it suspect, but hesitate; I would rather increase than diminish this lovely aptitude of a spirit genuinely young, this transparency of soul, this lambent cordiality — which, if the young have not, they have lost a section of true life, they have never been innocent — they are corrupt by anticipation, they have become prematurely old. But yet I would indicate a danger which lies in life, before the wisest and the best of the young. At any period of life, we see others much through the medium of ourselves, and never more so than in the first period. We cannot suppose, that they are otherwise than we are, and we feel that we would deal by all with openness, candor, generosity, and justice. We have not yet learned what effect life may have upon us; we know not how it may complicate our spirits, how it may vulgarize, soil, and debase us. Poverty or wealth, disappointment, trouble, betrayal, the discovery of insincere and hollow men, have not yet tried us, — if things have any good seeming, we take them for even better than they seem, and we price them with our own exaggerated estimate. But, some time, discovery will come, and though many may stand the test of years, yet some will prove but worthless. It is then, if we have not ourselves turned out castaways, that we may be tempted to give up our trust, and cease to have human faith. But this we must not do. The cynic is worse than the dupe; and, though we should have been disappointed in every individual with whom we have ever held intercourse, confidence in our Maker imposes confidence in our kind.

Take another error — as to feelings — and this is

an error peculiar to no part of life. If we are conscious of no malice, we often fancy that we can inflict no hurt. Our feelings are, upon the whole, charitable, humane, pitiful. We would not for all the gold of earth say a word that is false or evil of a fellow-creature, and much less be guilty towards him in any deliberate action. We are confident and without presumption, that, in the mass of our intentions, we have a benignant spirit; so far from causing a brother ill, we would do and bear much to cause him good, even though our enemy, if his need required, he should drink of our cup, and eat of our bread, and have shelter in our home. In friendship we would be disinterested, in affection devoted, in neighborly relations benevolent and blameless.

Why then should we curb these feelings, which are prompted so well by their native instincts? What need have they of government or of correction? Frequently, they need restraint and watchfulness because they are thus generally kind, because they are on that account so little suspected. For, notwithstanding all this amiability, there may be towards those who are near us and about us, no small quantity of peevishness, crossness, general ill-humor. Those called good-natured people do, often, unknowingly,. wittingly also, leave deep wounds — all the deeper, if they possess our affection or esteem. It is no excuse to say, that their irritation is quickly over — but so may not be the pain. A trigger may be pulled in a second, but the soul returns back never. Even dearest friends will sometimes irritate each other in a sort of levity. They make, on occasions, a play of torment; but, often the result is tragic and fatal. Why should friends ever speak lightly of tormenting one another. Not for any purpose can this be safely done. "It cannot and it will not come to good."

We have too many real trials to meet without amateur ones. We have too many wounds from those who care not for our pain — from those, indeed, who design our pain, to need any to be given us in sport, or at the hands of those, who, if they knew it, would be greatly grieved by the pain which they had caused. Amidst, as we are, too palpable ills, and vexations, and perplexities — amidst the wear and tear of years, the death of hopes, the shadows of present and coming troubles — amidst the pullings and tuggings of action and of labor, we can none of us afford to bear supererogatory infliction. It is a tax not set down in the tariff of affection. It is an overcharge in the commerce of friendship. It is an extra item added to the demand made upon forbearance, after the account has been discharged and our means are exhausted. It is an expense not foreseen upon our journey, and for which we have made no provision. In any way considered, it is as troublesome as it is unnecessary, and it ought not to have existence.

I have thus confined my remarks to instances which scarcely amount to the most ordinary difficulties or dangers of character, which yet, if entirely overlooked, may lead to failure, confusion and sorrow. I have thus confined myself, that the principle which I would urge in not being connected with any extreme illustration, may the more commend itself to sober judgment. But, how greatly further might I have gone, and still be not near to an extreme case. How negligent we all are, in allowing our minds to lie waste, or our unchecked feelings to overgrow them with noxious weeds, some waking hours of sad experience reveal to the most careless. If with the happiest constitution from nature, and the best position from circumstances, we yet need to constantly revise and to correct our tendencies, to turn every influence to its best use, what necessity is ours if our nature is of stubborn material, and our circumstances hard and unfavorable. But there is no reason even, then, to despair, no reason even to be discouraged. From such natures and out of such circumstances have been reared some of the characters that have most adorned and dignified humanity. It is easier to shape wood than marble, and marble than bronze — but bronze when moulded, is more lasting even than marble. But, the coarse and rugged granite, which had once been thought fit only to pile up in huge edifices stone upon stone, it has been discovered can, by the skilful carver, be made to take impression of the most beautiful and affecting sentiments. There is no occasion that I should apply, with any formal explanations, these examples in their analogies to character.

But, to what end is this discipline? The present question, as the former, I meet, or rather amplify by another, and that is, What is life for? The end of discipline is to make life that for which it is given. By deciding what that is, we determine at once the purpose of life, and the direction of its culture — moral and spiritual. Life then is for action, for work, for action and for work in the order of duty and of goodness.

True progress in life, therefore, is moral more than intellectual, the improvement of the inward being more than success in the external career. Not that I deny the importance of intellectual attainment and outward comfort. By no means would I depreciate them. In certain degrees, they are necessary, in general, to refinement and elevation of character, and, if they add nothing to the worth of virtue, they add much to its grace. The truth however, should never be concealed, that low states of ignorance and destitution expose life to moral evils, to mental degradation, and to social inefficiency. This is spoken in no spirit of contempt, but in that of profound sympathy and conviction.

That is a most infatuated idealism, a most blinded and perverted kind of religion, which can deny the hopeless darkness and grossness, in which unrelieved indigence and ignorance may place the soul. That soul may be as dead in the throng of a Christian city, as in the depths of a heathen desert. It is all but mockery to go to such souls, with a text of Scripture, and expect the miracle of a spiritual resurrection in the midst of their hunger and their filth. No, I insist, that to raise souls out of such conditions, or to keep them out of such, are, in the order of humanity and God, essential to any life above the most wretched and the most gloomy. Every effort, therefore, in this direction in men, for themselves or for others, is to be commended.

As little is it to be doubted that social appearances that imply prevailing competence, industry, and peace, are indexes to a correspondent prevalence of morality and religion. My observations were comparative and applied to ordinary circumstances, and, in this case, they are true; the best progress is moral more than intellectual, inward more than outward. It is not in the outward life the power acts which keeps the world safe. It is in the bosoms of the good, who though never idle, care little to be known. They are silent, but they are not thence in palsy. They are unnoticed, but they are not on that account unfelt. They are inspiring, they are active, but it is as the leaven in the three measures of meal, entering into the hearts around them in quiet influences — shaping the habits of those near them by the noiseless energy of example, and working in the community by that hidden force, which, at the same time, holds it together and carries it onward.

Life, I repeat, is for work. Man must work. That is certain as the sun. But he may work grudgingly, or he may work gratefully; he may work as a man, or he may work as a machine. He cannot always choose his work, but he can do it in a generous temper, and with an up-looking heart. There is no work so rude, that he may not exalt it; there is no work so impassive, that he may not breathe a soul into it; there is no work so dull, that he may not enliven it. Every work has its mystery in the understanding, of which the worker has pre-eminence. Every work has its conditions, reasons, and relations, in the comprehending of which the agent has his own sphere of power. In the degree, too, that a man finds dignity in his work, he has dignity in himself. Each part of a man needs to do a work, and each part of a man needs a work to be done for it. There is work by the body and for it; there is work by the mind and for it.

Each stage of a man needs a work, and each stage of a man needs a work to be done for it; childhood, youth, maturity, old age. It is the same in circle beyond circle of our social humanity. There is work in and from the home; there is work in and from the neighborhood; there is work in and from the state; there is work which goes out to the race; there is work which acts from generation to generation — all works merging in the work of Providence, which, itself, merges in the work that upholds the universe. No man then is base who does a true work, for true action is the highest being. No man is miserable that does a true work, for right action is the highest happiness. No man is isolated who does a true work, for useful action is the highest harmony — it is the highest harmony with nature and with souls — it is living association with men — and it is practical fellowship with God. Life being thus for work, it is, of consequence, for reward. But the reward is *in* the life, and not out of it. It is not *for* the life as a matter of merit — but is *of* the life, as a matter of necessity. It is not wages, but consciousness, and just as consciousness lives in thought and feeling, reward lives in virtue.

Happiness, therefore, is not the end of duty, it is a constituent of it. It is in it and of it; not an equivalent but an element. Make happiness once directly an end, and then duty there is none. There may be prudence, there may be expediency, but there is no duty. Nay, make happiness once an end, and you are sure to miss it. Can you call to mind any individual who studied his own happiness, that was ever happy? Can you call to mind any individual who labored for duty, that was ever really unhappy? I care not how false his idea of duty may have been; in fidelity to it, he has had peace. But the more his idea is pure, benevolent, generous, fruitful of wholesome practice, must it fill, and raise, and gladden him. The man that intends only his own happiness defeats his intention. The man that intends right, gains the object for which he does not strive. Reward, I repeat, is not arbitrary, it is inherent. It may not be marked until the work is done, but it was in the very doing of the work, and out of that doing it has come. Good deeds or evil deeds may, to the senses, appear equally prosperous and equally abortive; but however concealed, good deeds have their reward, and however delayed, evil deeds have their retribution.

By the discipline of which I have been speaking, I do not mean any formal schooling, or any mechanical training. Too much, already, there is of these in the world. I mean that which results from the inward action of the life itself, that, in fact, which constitutes experience. We are not to wait *to be*, in preparing to be. We are not to wait *to do*, in preparing to do, but to find in being and doing preparation for higher being and doing. Affections, friendships, pleasures, amusements are parts of this discipline, as well as moral vigilance and self examination — success as well as adversity, joy as well as sorrow.

But sorrow is the noblest of all discipline. Our nature shrinks from it, but it is not the less for the greatness of our nature. It is a scourge, but there is healing in its stripes. It is a chalice, and the drink is bitter, but strength proceeds from the bitterness. It is a crown of thorns, but it becomes a wreath of light on the brow which it has lacerated. It is a cross on which the spirit groans, but every Calvary has an Olivet. To every place of crucifixion there is likewise a place of ascension. The sun that was shrouded is unveiled, and heaven opens with hopes eternal to the soul, which was nigh unto despair. Even in guilt, sorrow has sanctity within it. Place a bad man beside the death-bed or the grave, where all that he loved is cold, we are moved, we are won by his affliction, and we find the divine spark yet alive, which no vice could quench. We cannot withhold our interest, and we are compelled to give him our respect.

Christianity itself is a religion of sorrow. It was born in sorrow, it was incarnate in sorrow, in sorrow it was tried, and by sorrow it was made perfect. The author of Christianity was a man of sorrows and acquainted with grief. Alone did he tread the wine-press of agony, until the last drop of torture was crushed out. Alone did he walk on the waves of affliction in the dark and stormy midnight of solitude and woe. With sensibilities so quick, so gentle; and so loving, with a perfect soul, to which wrong or wickedness must have caused unspeakable pain, yet to which the depths of wrong and wickedness were exposed; with sympathies alive to the smallest suffering, and yet which clasped in their wide embrace all humanity in its wants and its capacities; heavy, indeed, was the burden which his spirit had to bear. Not on one occasion only, but often, we conceive him bathed all over with the cold sweat of a terrible anguish, — often we may hear him exclaim, "My soul is sorrowful, exceeding sorrowful, sorrowful even unto death."

It was for such a being that humanity waited; out of the depths of its gloom, of doubt, of suffering and of sin, the heart of humanity cried for such a being, and in the fullness of time he came. Humanity looked up bewildered to the stars, it looked down weeping to the grave; but the stars were cold, and the grave was silent. With passionate supplications, with tears and blood, it besought reply to its deep sad questionings. But heaven and earth were mute to its petitions. At last a being was given to it, who understood the secret of its grief, and who solved the mystery of its fears; who spoke out of its own affections and to them; who, enduring its trials to the utmost, with the comfort of divine truth, bestowed the help of divine companionship. Distinctively, Christ was a man of sorrows, and, distinctively Christianity is a religion for the sorrowful. It is by affliction that the need of it is felt; it is by affliction that its innermost meaning is apprehended. Even the pardon which it proclaims, the mercy which it reveals, descends only on the tribulations of repentance. It is a religion which brings the soul into communion with solemn things on every side of it, and into most intimate communion with itself. It is a religion which, in giving the soul an ideal of faultless excellence, humbles and chastens it, in the presence of the holiness by which it is elevated and sanctified.

It awes by the majesty of its truths, it agitates by the force of its compunctions, it penetrates the heart by the tenderness of its appeals, and it casts over the abyss of thought, the shadow of its eternal grandeur. Nor is this all. It reveals such views of this thronged world, such views of those who throng it, as often to deepen reflection into sadness.

But this sadness is exalting. It is the baptism by which every man who lives profoundly, is introduced into his greater life. Since Christ wept over Jerusalem, the best and bravest, who have followed him, in good will and good deeds, have commenced their mission, like him, in suffering, and not a few of them, like him, have closed it in blood. Sorrow is not to be complained of, it is to be accepted. It has godliness in its power, it has joy within its gloom, and though Christianity is a religion of sorrow, it is not less a religion of hope ; it casts down in order to exalt, and, if it tries the spirit by affliction, it is to prepare it for beatitude.

PRAYER AND PASSION.

Luke xi. 3.

GIVE US DAY BY DAY OUR DAILY BREAD.

I have selected from the Lord's prayer the most lowly of its petitions for my text. It suggests to me a contrast between the spirit of prayer and the spirit of passion, in relation to the things of this life. It is on such contrast that I would at present enlarge.

"Give us day by day our daily bread." This is the desire of simple, of necessary want; and, so far as it is such, it is the universal prayer of living nature. It goes up for ever, from all regions of earth's animate existence; it is a grand, perpetual supplication, sounding through land, through ocean, and through air. What a mighty congregation is that which calls on God for supply, in which supply their life consists! And how wonderfully, how sublimely, how carefully, how mercifully is that supply administered! The whole universe is made to contribute to it. Earth out of her bosom, the sea out of its depths, the clouds out of their fullness, the stars from their height, the sun in the sweep and the changes of his glory, all are constituted ministries of beneficence to the lowliest wants of the lowliest creatures. And in order to conceive some faint idea as to the extent and power of those ministries, only suppose them for a short season suspended, and then try to imagine the compass and the terror of desolation that would ensue. Let even but one kind of food fail in a single nation, and a wail is heard over the world, which no distance can silence, which no boundaries can shut out, or hinder from wringing the hearts of the most remote with pity and alarm. What then would that state be, in which the air should move only to wither, the sun shine only to burn, and the clouds rain down only to deluge or to chill. It is a picture, which, could it be fully and clearly drawn, might make an angel tremble.

But while we shudder at such a state, even as a fancy, what gratitude should be ours to Him, to whose unceasing goodness we owe it, that it is not a reality? Yes, it is God to whom all creatures call, and it is God who hears that call and answers it with bounty. "Consider the ravens, for they neither sow nor reap; which neither have storehouse nor barn, and God feedeth them." And man, too, is not less dependent than the ravens; for what would all the skill of men amount to, what would all their toils be worth, if God did not bless them, if he did not give them rain from heaven, and fruitful seasons, filling their heart with food and gladness? What would all their planting, all their watering result in, if God did not give the increase? And yet it is not the less true, that though the hand of God scatters plenty over his world, that numbers of his rational children pine in it for want of bread; that numbers are in the dark places of hunger and destitution, weeping in their misery, dying in their famine; babes withering on the bosoms of their mothers; fathers with their manly strength bent down by fasting, and bent down by contemplating the sufferings of those whom they cannot rescue, or whom they would die to save, even by their own privations. I cannot think, whatever philosophers may assert, that this is any necessity in the creation of a gracious Father. I cannot but regard it as, on the whole, the effect of sin and selfishness; sin often on the side of the poor themselves, and selfishness on the part of others. And this very sin of the poor, how often is it produced by want, and when not produced, how often is it increased, perpetuated, aggravated, by want.

To what crimes will not hunger alone frequently drive men. When a stout man who would work beholds his wife pale with long and involuntary abstinence;

when he beholds the emaciated faces of his children turned upon him with a sort of discontented wonder that he does not relieve them; when he feels nothing about him but dreariness and cold; and death, in ghastly leanness, is squatted on his hearth, between fever and famine; it is only by a holy strength which is more than human, that a man, in such circumstances, can keep himself from madness and from becoming a fiend or a brute. There is nothing marvellous in the fact, that many fall before temptations that are so dreadful; the true wonder is, that any can resist and stand. There is nothing marvellous in the fact, that out of such circumstances should come thefts, falsehoods, robberies, the destruction in numbers of all manly integrity, the blight of all womanly purity.

A most comprehensive petition is this, then, though we should use it only in relation to physical existence, when we use it in the Christian spirit, not alone in reference to the wants of the individual, but in reference also to the wants of collective humanity. Then we do in effect pray for the sun to shine, and for the rain and dew to fall, and for the seasons to roll, so that earth shall bring forth her increase, and that God, even our God, shall give them all his blessing; we do in effect pray for the sustainment of nature, and for the preservation of all life;

we do, in effect, pray for the good order of society, for wisdom in the rulers, and for virtue in the people, for misgovernment may bring want upon the most fertile regions, and idleness and vice cannot escape from destitution amidst the fullest plenty; we do, in effect, pray for the distribution of needful supply to all nations and all conditions of men; if not by abundant harvests, by abundant charity, by the grace of heaven in the heart, so that he who has much shall impart to him that has little, and he who has little to him that has none.

"Give us day by day our daily bread," is the desire of moderation. It most assuredly cannot, or does not, mean any savage simplicity, or any ascetic self-denial. It would not teach men to long for nothing more than animal subsistence. It would not exclude other and more ardent and more intense longings of man's nature. For observe our Lord's own precept: "Man does not live by bread alone, but by every word that proceedeth out of the mouth of God." Man's life, therefore, does not consist in the satisfaction of his mere animal wants, nor does his highest and heavenliest spiritual life imply that he must reduce these animal wants to their very lowest requirements. Certainly greater words come out of the mouth of God, than those which speak to us of self-preservation, or than those which urge us by the irresistible instincts of hunger and of thirst; and as we may laudably desire more on the animal side of our nature, than that which shall merely satisfy hunger and thirst, so, on the other side, we may laudably desire something more than that which relieves it from anguish, or leaves it in apathy. It is perfectly right for us to wish for whatever can give a calm and complete replenishment to the whole of our nature; but sometimes we must limit that wish, and become obedient to our circumstances.

Yet, are there enjoyments, without which there can be no exalted life, which it is not only right to desire, but which, not to desire, implies a most debased and grovelling existence; which, moreover, to desire is to possess. There is, for instance, a wish for those sympathies from our fellows, in their several relations to us, which are the food of our best affections. There is a longing after the ideal and the beautiful in life and in nature. Above all, I will not say *there is*, but there should be a yearning for supplies from heaven, from God, for the strength and the refreshment of our spirits, for growth and power in every good and holy thing. I have said, that to desire such blessings is to possess them, and is it not so? What really generous and loving heart ever fails of sympathy, in the general compass of its experience? True, it will have trials and sadness, and oftentimes it will seem nigh to breaking amidst jarring and antagonist elements, but such a heart in its own pure strength, will surmount them, and even change them into a placid atmosphere, which will glow with heat and brightness from the flame of its charities.

When our simple wants are met, we then need but tranquil souls to know that we can own, if we have an inward feeling of what is grand and fair, an immense wealth of beauty. And for this, there is no occasion that we have access to galleries of art, or be surrounded by the sublimity or grace of architecture ; it is enough that we have humanity and animals, that we have a goodly earth and a glorious heaven. And as to influence, aid from God, they may be ours, whenever our souls will have them. We are embosomed in his mercy, and it is only the darkness of our own sins and passions which shuts out the light of goodness by which we are surrounded. He calls to us with perpetual voice ; He is about us with an everlasting Presence ; He solicits our affections by unceasing and unfailing benefits ; but when out of harmony with his laws, we have no apprehension of his nature, we have no spiritual hearing for his voice, we have no spiritual sight for his Presence, and our affections are insensible to his benefits. If we seek Him in simple and pure desire, He will be abundantly revealed to us ; and once in communion with the Perfect, we have the full inheritance of Peace.

I have quoted our Lord's precept, I will now refer to his example. There is no ascetism in his character. His life was a life of beautiful proportions. His tastes were simple, but not narrow or exclusive. He did not shun men's company or their festivals, nor did he cast ever a shade upon their joys when he appeared among them. He came eating and drinking; and yet impiety itself cannot associate his life with that of the senses. There is a halo of sanctity thrown around it, which the fiercest unbelief dares not to sully with a taint of accusation. His love was accorded to whatever things were lovely, to children, to birds, to flowers; and bread was not more the daily nourishment of his body, than the good and the beautiful were the daily nourishment of his soul. And, also, did he ask for sympathy, for friendship; deeply did he feel it, fervently he blessed it, and cordially did he pay it back; he, too, amidst daily struggle and daily trial, yearned for human hearts to support him in hours of despondency, and to come near to him in hours of solitude. He whose intercommunion with God was such as man had never had before, was yet most widely human; and, while agitated by none of the lower or ruder passions, we behold him filled with the strongest and the most sensitive affections. Wonderful, that one whom all men class with a common brotherhood, as feeling in him the amplitude of their nature, should reveal their nature to them only in blameless excellence, and in unimpeachable virtue. He had its *wants*, but not its sins; and he was identified with it in every prayer, except the prayer for pardon.

" Give us day by day our daily bread," is the desire of faith, of trust. It is the desire of faith, of that principle of the spiritual man, by which the soul has cognizance of a life higher than that of the appetites or the senses; of that principle in the soul, by which it discerns a good, nobler than any physical enjoyment, and wants deeper and more lasting than any physical needs. As for our body, its existence is transient, and so are its requirements; its existence is from day to day. Let not this, therefore, be the matter to us of the most absorbing and the most permanent anxiety. " The life is more than meat." Why then give such disproportionate care for the meat that perisheth, and think so little of the life, which shall endure for ever? Gather as we may, the treasure we amass here will soon avail us nothing. If not otherwise wrenched from us, Time is a thief that approacheth, and a moth that corrupteth; but there is a treasure in heaven, where no thief approacheth, neither moth corrupteth. Seek first, and seek always, the kingdom of God, and his righteousness, the kingdom of God within you, above you; before you; seek an inward life, an upward life, a growing, a progressive life; a life devoted to the right, and then the transient sustenances which your temporary wants require, will not fail you.

And, truly, when we ponder on the subject seriously, not merely in the spirit of faith, but according to the dictates of a practical judgment, we are forced to wonder that we should be so vexed, and fretted, and discontented, by things as fleeting as wreaths of mist, things that pass away as quickly, and that leave as little trace. When a few years are over, where shall those things be? "Sufficient unto the day is the evil thereof." And this is a sentiment of trust as well as a sentiment of faith. As by faith we discern the nature of those objects, and so learn justly to estimate them, by trust, we have filial confidence in God, who alone can give them, or withhold. We rely upon Him as the paternal provider for all his children, and to Him we look as to a Father, to give us, while we are here, such things as he knoweth that we need. But this is no indolent trust; it is no trust that makes sanctity of idleness, and beatitude of apathy. It is not a trust which would set aside industry, or justify improvidence. On the contrary, it is a trust which prompts to useful action, and leads to careful foresight. Knowing that God works by means, the Christian expects a blessing only where the means are used. And just in the degree that he uses the proper means, and uses them wisely, will he be humble in his confidence; for he who acts rashly, and yet looks for a safe result, is not pious but presuming; and he who does not act at all, yet hopes to be as well as if he labored, is a sluggard and a fool.

The true Christian is an active man and a wise man; and he is all the more active and the more wise, the more that he relies upon divine power and divine aid; for such reliance endows his plans and labors with a constant energy. He is not disturbed by solicitude, he is not enfeebled by care; he pursues his course in peace; he does all that prudence suggests, all that duty requires; and then leaving the result to God, he possesses his soul in patience and in peace. Moderate in his desires, believing in his spirit, if the world's goods are given, he is thankful for them as means of virtue; if they are refused, he is resigned, and is thankful still for an opportunity of discipline; if they are taken from him, he meets adversity with a manly fortitude. He knows equally how to abound, and how to suffer loss; in any station, how to be content; how to be content, not from the absence of aspiration, but the greatness of it; an aspiration, that looks up to such heights of glory, and is filled with such a majesty of hope, that the crags and thorns by which our earthly feelings are tired and wounded, appear but as shadows on a grass-plot; and the disappointments by which they may be for a time embittered, but as the vexations of a child.

I have thus endeavored, but with very inadequate expression, to state what the spirit of prayer, as our Lord teaches, is, regarding the desires of the present condition of existence. They imply the demands of the physical life, in its absolute wants, and they exclude not its moderate enjoyments; neither do they repel the proper culture and lawful indulgence of refined and ideal tastes; and they not only accord with all the purer affections and sympathies of our nature, but strengthen, enlarge, and elevate them. It follows, as a matter of the simplest inference, that desires regulated by such a spirit, will be liberal and beneficent. The Christian does not pray for an isolated supply. He does not say, give *me*, but give *us*, our daily bread. He does not desire that *his* good shall be any other man's evil; and the good which is committed to his care, it is his happiness to distribute.

It follows, as a matter of equally simple inference that desires regulated by such a spirit can never be cruel, inhuman, or unjust. They can never wish for the infliction of pain or suffering on others; they can never deliberately ask for what belongs to others; they can never voluntarily hold what belongs to others; and such desires, therefore, can have neither affinity nor alliance with the continuance or extension of any remediable misery among the children of men, with the origin or perpetuation of any known wrong in the world. The only desires which we can dare to present in prayer, are simple, modest, pure, generous, humane, just; and whether for the things of this life or the other. If they are of a contrary temper, we then should find the heavens a canopy of brass against our cry; our supplications might be fit addresses to Mammon and to Moloch, but not to the Father of Jesus; for our feeling to Him, could not then be that of faith and trust, but that of outrage and blasphemy.

I have occupied so much time on desire, as governed by the spirit of prayer, that little space is left me to illustrate the contrast to it, of desire as governed by the spirit of passion.

The passions are exorbitant. I speak, of course, of the passions in the popular use of the term, as implying desires which seek mainly their own gratification, without reference to the principles that limit them for the good of the individual and the good of the community. No passion, thus considered, is ever content within the most complete circle of its natural enjoyment. It is ever trying to push out that circle to a wider and wider circumference; it fancies that it does so, but such fancies are deceits; it only destroys itself in struggles against an immovable barrier, or goes round and round it in the insensate routine of habit. That barrier is fixed by God and nature, and every effort to stir it is vain; not so are the threatenings against them, for the penalties are inevitable. The passions are selfish. This is the point from which they depart, and to which they ever and again return; to enrich self, to gratify self, or to exalt self; and to one or other of these motives separately, we may trace the vices of individual characters; and to the action of them all collectively, most of the sins and inhumanities which blacken society and curse the world. When once passion takes full possession of the heart, the whole man is absorbed; and all his better faculties must bend before tyranical desire. Such desire is blind and insensible to every moral consideration; it loses respect and pity for others, and it would subject them as instruments, or destroy them as opponents; it has no inlet for truth, it defies argument, it despises reason, it scouts at obligation; it tramples upon any claim opposed to its own absorbing monopoly; it so indurates the conscience, that the truest impulses of moral instinct, the most impressive pleadings of charity and justice, appear to it but as mockery and babble.

The passions, thus considered, are utterly irreligious; they chill the religious feeling even into moral atheism. When once the authority of God is practically set aside, when the supremacy of his laws is practically resisted, when reverence to his character has no testimony in the soul and no evidence in the life, when the rectitude of his government is silently felt, not as freedom but as hardship; the formal acknowledgment of his existence, is little better than a fraud upon men, and an insult upon heaven. The passions so crowd the temple of the heart with idols, that there is no room in it for the presence of the true and only God to be recognized or worshipped.

Let me briefly illustrate this brief review; and that common and obvious division, which makes *wealth*, *pleasure*, *power*, the leading objects of human passion, will be sufficiently accurate for our space and purpose.

The passions, I have asserted, are exorbitant. What man that has given his heart to gain is content within the most ample wants of nature, ay, or within any of the possible cravings of luxury? Let him have as much as will secure abundance to the most protracted life, let him have as much as will surround the largest family with affluence, let him have as much as will entail idleness and unthrift on a long posterity, still, he is not content; and the zeal of this passion is eating him up; it will not satisfy him, and will not let him rest. It is as the sword, that can slay forever, and yet not be tired; it is as the fire, that can flame forever, and burn the more, the more that it consumes; it is as the daughters of the horse-leech that keep always crying, give, give, give, and cry still more loudly as the more they get, give, give; it is as the GRAVE, that devours always, and devours all things, but is never full.

I have suggested that the passions are selfish. Take witness of those who devote themselves to pleasure, where can you find selfishness more intense and more complete? Nor, so far as our position is concerned, does it much signify, whether the desires be those of sensuality, or those of vanity, one or the other, they are not the less the movings of selfishness. How many consume upon their worst inclinations, wealth that would bless thousands. How many blight and desolate even in their own homes, and yet, while they gratify, ruin themselves! Look out upon the world; behold the vice that curses it, the wickedness that profanes it; comprehend, if you can, the devastation, the guilt, the misery, the insanity, the godless livings, the hopeless dyings, the endless varieties of sorrow that turn the crowded places of civilization so much into social gehennas, — all these are the achievements of passion active only for pleasure and for self. From the selfish spirit working thus in its coarser forms, we naturally avert our thoughts. Yet, how would vanity be startled, — vanity which walks in the pride of propriety, in the gaud of distinction, in the ease of station, in the gaze of fashion, — if we were to tell IT, that this hateful principle, self-gratification, lurks underneath its tinsel glitter; that this fearful cancer of the spirit, though covered with jewels and reputation, is not the less deadly.

I have said the passions are irreligious; but why should I extend my illustrations, or say any thing upon the inordinate desire for power? What right, human or divine, does it acknowledge? In the individual or the nation, in whom it rules, it takes no heed of God but to blaspheme him, or of man but to crush him.

We will not continue farther this tone of reflection, but close with such instruction as the subject can afford us. Every prayer implies a duty, this prayer implies many. I will mention only two: self-denial and beneficence. It implies self-denial. It is but justice to others to govern desire within due bounds; for in whatever degree we exceed these by intention, we commit a wrong against our brethren in purpose; and in whatever degree we exceed these bounds by actions, we do them an injury in fact. To restrain desire, is wisdom to ourselves. If we trust the passions, they will deceive us. The passions come to us with fair promises, but they reverse these promises into the most galling disappointments. The passions come to us blooming and with smiles, but ere we know them long, we see them to be haggard. They come to us as suitors, but they carry bonds behind them ; they offer to clothe us in rich attire, yet, in a little while, we discover there was poison in their folds, or they hang around us as filthy rags.

Let us look at the reality of things, and seek for the moderation of nature and of God, and, in the spirit which aims at no excess, we will learn to be beneficent. If the good Father grants us our daily bread, let us eat it in content; if he gives us more, let us share it with a cheerful temper. Let those who abound in wealth, abound also in works. Many every where are in need, which a very little of your superfluity would relieve. The destitute are in all places, in all times; scarcely a community so prosperous, that has not some to touch the pity of the generous. Think, then, with eloquent Isaac Barrow, that " 't is the naked man's apparel which you shut up in your presses, and which you exorbitantly ruffle and flaunt in ; that 't is the needy person's gold and silver which you closely hide or spend idly, or put to useless use." Then deal thy bread to the hungry, and raiment to the uncovered, not more as an act of mercy than an act of justice. If these be not near you, they are afar; and, if you cannot do it in your own persons, you can by your agents.

But do not limit the precept to its literal interpretation; give it a spiritual meaning, and make it a spiritual fact by a spiritual application. There are some whom you can feed with truth or support with consolation, or encourage with sympathy; there are some souls which you can cheer; there are some hands which you can strengthen; there are some eyes which you can brighten. In this we can all participate: where we are not able to work ourselves, we will help those who are working; and even if that be not in our power, we will bid them God speed, and wish them a blessing on their way. And as day by day we ask our Father to give us bread,— not the bread alone, which springs from the ground, but the bread also which comes down from heaven,— the bread of truth, the bread of freedom, the bread of universal charity, the bread of life,— all men shall be included in that holy aspiration — the deep desire that all men may partake with ourselves the best gifts of God, shall mingle with the prayer and sanctify it; and soul shall unite itself to soul in consenting supplication, until a congregation which no man can number, shall put it forth, not as a sound upon the lips, but as the breathings of the spirit in a cloud of ever-ascending and ever-dwelling incense; and the Creator will listen to his faithful people, and will pour these bounties down, in showers as bright as the sun, as wide as the earth, — and, as the angels sang first at the birth of the gospel, they will sing, then, at its triumph.

TEMPER.

MARK ix. 50.

HAVE PEACE ONE WITH ANOTHER.

It is truly astonishing how little our moral reflections dwell upon our tempers; how seldom the errors of it impress us with any strong regrets or penitence. We rarely blame ourselves on their account, and we further presume that others also ought not to blame us. We value a good reputation beyond riches, and for fame or fortune, we think no exertions too great; but as to the regulations of temper, not to say that we rarely esteem it a duty, we rarely give it a thought. We do not reflect on the space of existence over which our temper spreads, and which it bathes in light or sows with thorns. We do not remember how passing cruel we may be without inflicting wounds or imprisonment, without either the dagger or the dungeon. We do not think that we are all creatures of sympathy, that we share each other's life, and that we have a power, all but boundless, to render each other happy or unhappy.

In the strength of our selfishness we too often forget the harshness of our words, the coldness or bitterness of our looks, and we care not for the deep and bleeding incisions which they leave behind them. We do not enough consider how much a gentle temper may be the evidence of a noble nature; and how much an ungentle one may be the shadowing forth of a dark and contracted soul: the moral beauty as well as moral strength that are implied in sweetness of spirit, and the moral hideousness that makes its dwelling in a bitter heart.

What is the difference in principle between the most cruel tyrant and the truest lover of his kind? It is temper. When your imagination forms to itself the idea of an angel or a fiend, what is still the difference? It is temper. And could you clothe the angel or the fiend in human shape, the most prominent characteristic in each would yet be temper. As to those also whom we once have known, who casually crossed our path, or walked along with us for years in this our pilgrimage, does not our involuntary memory turn to their habits of temper? When their bones are in ashes, when many of their good and bad deeds have gone into forgetfulness, again and again they live to us in the recollection of their tempers; we see again their benign or clouded looks, we hear again their kind or harsh expressions. We can forget an act of malice, however dark, but we cannot forget that which for years has eaten as iron into our souls. We may be ungrateful for an act of goodness, however generous, but we are unable to dissolve the charm which, through many days of peace and charity, spread its light around us. We consider not how much temper enters into daily life; how it penetrates the whole surface of existence; that it is in our daily employments, in our general society, in our homes, around our hearths; that it gives sweetness to the dinner of herbs, or turns luxury to the food of misery.

It would be impossible to enumerate and classify all the failings of temper, for they are as many as there are peculiarities of human character. The general constitution of the mind gives the cast to temper; and therefore the varieties of temper must be infinite. We shall, however, glance at bad temper in a few of its most evil forms, and we can only do so in some of their broader distinctions. There are the *violent*, strong in coarse and selfish passions, unable to bear any contradiction to a stubborn will, and, as the case may be, they keep in strife a nation or a household. The temper of this species is the prime element in the tyrannic character whether of greater or smaller dimensions, whether of a family or an empire. Give it a religious direction, and it makes the bigot, the fanatic, and the persecutor.

Give it power, and it will again open the Inquisition, or rekindle the fires of the stake. In more calm and respectable orders of society, wherever decorum at the least has rule, this disposition can have but rare exhibition; but in other grades of life, in which character has one rude formation and expression, no restraint, it has a ravaging and a fearful existence. It grieves one to the very heart to know that a low, barbarous and ruffian nature, sulky, obtuse and unforbearing, can fill to the brim the measure of calamity, that the few he has near him can endure; that the home he calls his castle, he can for others make a dungeon; that the liberty of which he boasts, he can make to them a bondage; that the power which should be their guardianship, he can make their terror: it grieves one, I say, to know that such a savage may exist in a free and Christian country; that he can heap sorrows without number on dependent and defenceless victims; that he can embitter their existence and bruise their hearts; that within his sphere of bounded tyranny, he can be as complete a despot as if he wore the crown of all the Russias — a cruel, fierce, and unmitigated despot.

There are, again, the *morose;* and the temper of this class as it has various forms, so it has likewise manifold sources. It may be founded in extreme self-consequence or in extreme self-dissatisfaction, and it may be evidenced in haughty contempt, or in silent and cold indifference. Such a temper constrains the spirit; it leaves the soul few social attractions and few generous desires; it throws gloom where there ought to be light, it withers the smile half-formed, it silences the word half-spoken, it robs action of loveliness, and takes all grace from speech; it has no soul of frank and generous appreciation; its natural element is to destroy rather than to create; it seems to live only to prove how much a rational creature may mistake the object of his existence, and how much pain one human creature may give to another without reaping any gain or pleasure to himself. The misery that violence inflicts, it inflicts openly — this does it silently: violence often feels its wrong — this never; violence has its moments of deep compunction and periods of sorrowful and gentle tenderness that almost atone for many of its worst injuries — but this austere reserve has no visitings of open-heartedness, and no times of refreshment. I have said that a violent temper makes the tyrant — this makes the cynic; I have said that a violent temper makes the fanatic — this makes the ascetic: if both, therefore, be equal in unkindness, the one is at least more coldly intolerable than the other.

Further, there are the *revengeful.* The others I have mentioned are commonly founded in pride, — this more frequently in vanity; pride can be magnanimous, can forget and can forgive, but wounded vanity remembers an offence forever, and seldom forgives it. To beings of this spirit, flattery is the very breath of their nostrils, the food of their life. Rough or disagreeable truth is not to be endured, but what then must be positive injustice? Sensitive at all points, such persons are hurt when you do not know it and could not intend it. Often you give a mortal stab when you but made a careless movement; they ponder over words and actions, until a mole-hill seems to be a mountain, and they revolve and revolve the thought so often, that an offence becomes fixed immovably in their imaginations; they catch the transgressor by the throat, and will not let him go, until he has paid the uttermost farthing. In this imperfect world, we have many failings and many provocations; but as we value the least fragment of a benign humanity, let us keep the spirit free from this most bitter dreg of earthly evils, this last and worst sin of a short-sighted and corrupted nature. O, let us, as we value our own heart's best and most godlike peace, as we value every moment of present tranquillity and of future hope, keep them free from anti-social, and hard, and unmerciful dispositions.

There are, moreover, the *discontented*. The temper of those is that which goes from Dan to Beersheba, and on every step of the way cries that all is barren. This is the one that sees little in man or in life with the open heart or the clear eye of enjoyment; this is the one that no society can please, that no character can suit, that no exertions can earn approval from, that no condition can satisfy; that is equally complaining, equally unhappy, equally dissatisfied, in prosperity or in poverty. For those of such spirit earth has no retreat, they can have no shelter and no refuge. Whither can they flee? The world is full of imperfections, and so are the men that live in it. If we have only sight for evils, they are abundant in every place and in all conditions; wherever we turn, if we will not look on aught but these, we must have aching heads and aching souls.

There are persons who seem even to delight in proving that there is in the world more of evil than of good, and more of what is baneful than what is beautiful. They take joy from prosperity, and they add more than its natural bitterness to poverty; in success they are without gratitude, in failure they are without patience or dignity, — to describe them in few words, they are always disappointed! The mountain or the plain, the city or the desert, soft skies or dark ones, are all equal to those who will not see the works of God with a single eye, and will not hear the words of man with an open ear. The glories of nature, or the glories of art, men, books, or business, — nothing can take from them the occasion to complain. No gleam from heaven can cheer their hearts, no sounds on earth can charm away their irritation. There is no benison in religion that can give them a contented peace ; they wither under a spiritual malady, they are not happy, and, stranger still, they scarcely would be happy. If this be thought an over-colored picture, turn to what we witness daily in life, to what we daily feel in our own minds, the peevish tempers which we all so constantly indulge, and in which we think it no harm to indulge, the remorseless and ungenerous pelutance with which we hurt our fellow-creatures, with which we make them suffer for any of our own small vexations or annoyances, — vexations or annoyances that we have brought upon ourselves, and which it is more than probable we fully merit. In this most unamiable temper we chill and disgust the best-intentioned friends; the movement of kindness is despised; the word of affection dies upon the lips of the utterer; a willingness to think wrong where it *is not*, to *exaggerate* where it is, predominates in such natures ; no devotion of attachment, no ardor of generosity, no zeal of love can conquer it. Child or servant lives but in slavery or fear, and often when most deserving receive most rebuke.

Brethren, if our souls are tortured with unknown sorrows, as many of them must be, — if we have griefs for which we have no speech, if we have cares with which we cannot trust the stranger, if we have thoughts and woes which we have no heart to tell even to our nearest friend ; yet let us not dishonor them, let us not desecrate them by distilling them into the venom of ungenial tempers, let us magnanimously endure them, let us be ourselves the martyrs of our own sufferings ; and if we cannot assuage them in our closets by weeping and by prayer, let us not embitter the lot of others by peevishness and by cynicism. If we cannot be cheerful, let us at least not be unamiable. If we cannot rejoice when others rejoice, let us not throw gall into the cup of pleasure which mortals here are permitted to taste, and which must so soon be emptied.

But to observe, as sometimes we all may, the face grow dark, and the tones become harsh, on account of some wretched trifle, some bubble that is to vanish in a moment, we wonder not it should be so, because they are Christians, but because they are rational creatures ; we wonder not because they give pain to brethren, but because they ruffle their own peace ; and all this for what to either was not worth a moment's trouble or a moment's annoyance.

To close the enumeration, we mention the *capricious ;*

and this is the worst, for it is the most uncertain. You have nothing on which to calculate, you have no means of refuge or of remedy. To the violent and morose, you may oppose patience, and thus disarm them; the haughty you may meet with humility, and haply subdue them; the discontented, you may learn not to notice; the peevish, if they are worth gaining, or that your duty teaches you to make the effort, you may at last gain by proofs of sincerity and tenderness; but of the capricious you have never the slightest security, neither for hatred nor for love. Gentle this hour, they are stern in the next, zealous and indifferent, kindly and severe, indulgent and vindictive, charitable and unmerciful; they run incessantly through all modes of feeling; they exhibit in no long periods of time, all possible contrasts of character; their evil is equally evanescent with their good, but you can never be armed for their evil, and you have no sooner felt their good, than you fear to lose it. At one time they would move heaven and earth to make you happy, and in the turn of a moment they would scarcely move a finger; at one time they would burden you with favors, and at others they heap on you their darkest dislike; to-day they offer you their friendship, and to-morrow they withdraw it, and both the offer and the withdrawal are equally without assignable or discoverable reason. Their will is their law; but if there be such a thing, their law is chance. They seem to have no settled rules in either their feelings or their actions, no defined order of character, and, therefore, you have no common principles on which to judge them, or by which to hold them. You feel near them, similarly to those who stand around an Eastern sultan's throne, — who at one moment bask in the smiles of his favor, but who are in hourly fear, he will give the nod which shall unsheath the sword of the executioner.

Those who are in immediate connection with the class that I have described, live in constant and painful alternation, in which there is no ease, or certainty or comfort; in which life is made such a mortal torture as scarcely to be endured; in which family dependence is a galling yoke, and the bread of toil is eaten in tears of bitterness. Servants in lands of liberty, can retreat, they can choose their masters, — but families, what can they do? Remain and suffer! Remain, endure, and be hopeless and helpless victims; remain, and for mere existence bear whatever those who rule their existence can heap upon them; remain, and have all the pangs of martyrdom, and none of its honors. We cannot always choose our lot, nor is it right to quarrel with the lot which is assigned us; but if it were permitted us, there are surely many things which we would prefer to constant irritation and to domestic tyranny. It were better to scoop a cave in an Arabian desert, and, as the old hermits did, diet on herbs and water, than to be under this irritable and cruel caprice, though we should have robes of purple and fare sumptuously every day; it were better to raise a tent in some woods of the far off and untrodden west; it were better to be amidst the wild and pathless prairies, and to take the red man's fate, to have freedom and peace, and communion with God amidst his most awful solitudes and his grandest works; than to be inmates of a palace in which ill temper were the presiding spirit. Duty might command us to bear, but inclination would never choose it.

I have thus endeavored to point out a few broad generalities. In such a subject, minuteness were impossible. We give no rules for cure, because we conceive all such rules inefficacious. Each one should know his own special temptation, and if he is at all to be corrected, from himself should come the remedy. It is vain to give rules and maxims; they are of no account, unless there is an inward feeling of imperfection, unless there is an earnest, a heartfelt, a conscientious spirit of sincerity: if these be in the mind, it will truly discover and most earnestly apply the very best means of moral progression. Still it is right for us to consider a few of the excuses which are alleged for ill temper. And when faults of temper are at all admitted, what are the excuses pleaded? Some plead natural constitution — they are betrayed, when they design it not, into wrong speaking, and into wrong doing. Some plead bodily illness or the misfortunes of life; want of health has thrown a cloud upon their spirits, or men have not dealt well with them, or fortune and the world have been rough and boisterous on their course. Some plead the errors of their previous training; they were not taught better, and they did not see better; they were furnished with no right principles, and they saw all wrong examples. Some plead provocations not to be resisted, and say that, to have been otherwise than they are, were to have been more than human. Some, unwilling to confess any fault, will maintain that their conduct is that which is just and necessary. This would, no doubt, be the largest class, when they reason with men: we hope they are not so, when they reason with their consciences; still at times, they must remember, that although man sees only the outside appearance, God judges the heart. But as to these or any other excuses, whilst we should be generous in admitting them for our brethren, we should be cautious in taking them to ourselves.

That physical constitution is at the root of many of

our faults, is not to be denied, but neither is it to be denied, that it has an influence on much of our excellence. We know there are those in earliest youth, whom all of us have had the means of discerning, confiding, faithful, charitable, ready to be pleased, unwilling to find fault; whilst others have been sharp, harsh, unkind, watchful, proud, and selfish. And seldom has it been that the later nature has been opposed to early promise. That natural disposition may cause moral derangement should not be denied, neither should it be excluded from the number of mitigating circumstances; that illness may depress, and misfortunes vex us, we are all too well experienced to be severe on those who have undergone them impatiently; that wrong education may leave faults which shall endure to latest hours of life, many of us have but too much reason to lament, and these faults may be far more sincerely lamented by those who commit them, than by those who condemn them; that great provocation — and much there certainly is in life — demands also charitable allowance, we have no reason and no wish to deny, when it calls forth a strong and indignant burst of passion.

But when we have made all the admission that justice demands and charity can grant, some serious considerations remain, after all, to be pondered. In what way do we use these excuses? How often do we advance them when there is no ground for any of them, when there is no illness, no adversity, no evil example, no evil communication, no resistance; when every word and will is law; when health, and prosperity, and pleasures, and hopes, and friendships, and smiles from heaven and from men, and obsequious attendance are all about us, or awaiting our command; when the miseries that strike others down have passed over us, and not touched us; when death, the lot of all, as yet has left our dwellings full; when as yet the destroying angel has never waved his sword over us, nor pierced our hearts, nor opened the sluices of our tears; how often then are we in bitter and unhappy moods, when there seems no human reason, but an infatuated perverseness.

And though all these excuses in part were true, how much in our self-love do we over-color them. We are our own advocates, and therefore we are not likely to be just or severe judges. But though they were entirely true, what of that? Is it not demanded of a moral and virtuous man to overcome temptation — to subdue difficulties? Will not the right-minded man, not to say the Christian, struggle against his natural infirmities, nor cease until he has secured a victory? If we were to act on all our merely natural emotions, moral reasoning must be put out of the question. Akin to the brutes, we should be driven by the force of impulse, and to this necessity we can attach neither praise nor censure. We call not the gentleness of the lamb, *virtue*, nor the fierceness of the tiger, *vice*. But man we expect to have a control over his sensations; we expect him to be a moral being, and if he looks to us not to reckon the wrong he has done, because he has done it in accordance with his sensations, he asks us in point of fact to strip him of his humanity. Similar reasoning applies to the other causes alleged, but not so directly. We cannot here go into the distinctions; enough is it to say, that we have seen them frequently overcome, and what has been done hitherto can be done again; what men *ought* to do, they *can* do, and all excuses to the contrary are but so many equivocations and sophistries for self-will.

It has been the misfortune of many to have received a false training, and to have witnessed unseemly examples; but they have cast off the incubus of their education, and been good in spite of their examples. It has been the misfortune of many to lie long and low in sickness; but it has been their glory and their blessing to be meek through all their pains. There have been those who have come to a poor and dependent old age, and yet preserved the affections of their hearts and the light of their spirits; there have been those who have seen their best expectations fail on the point of fulfilment, and their best contrived plans turned into vanity, and their honest exertions defeated, and nothing but losses, struggles and fears made the daily and nightly companions of their thoughts; who have yet well endured their lot, and valiantly fought their fight, who could shake off the dark fiend that haunts the afflicted, who would not hear the voice of the tempter, and cursed neither God nor man. There have been those who, in the teeth of the most violent provocation, thought forbearance more noble than contest; who learned and practised the magnanimous lesson, "not to return evil for evil," and who preferred rather to endure injury than to inflict it; who would have chosen rather to pray with Christ on his cross, than to reign with the wrong-doer on his throne. All these excuses are futile and unsound. We must not deceive ourselves by them. Evil tempers can be corrected, and they ought.

They can be corrected. Who is he that says, he cannot help being angry, or sullen, or peevish? I tell him he deceives himself. We constantly avoid being so, when our interest or decorum requires it, when we feel near those whom we know are not bound to bear our whims, or who will resent them to our injury; but what strangers will not endure, we cast upon our friends. That temper can be corrected, the world proves by thousands of instances. There have been those who set out in life with being violent, peevish, discontented, irritable, and capricious, whom thought, reflection, effort, not to speak of piety, have rendered, as they became mature, meek, peaceful, loving, generous, forbearing, tranquil, and consistent. It is a glorious achievement, and blessed is he who attains it.

But taking the argument to lower ground, which I do unwillingly, you continually see men controlling their emotions, when their interest commands it. Observe the man who wants assistance, who looks for patronage, how well, as he perceives coldness, or hesitation, does he crush the vexation that rises in his throat, and stifles the indignation that burns for expression. How will the most proud and lofty descend from their high position, and lay aside their ordinary bearing, to earn a suffrage from the meanest hind. And surely those who hang around us in life, those who lean on us, or on whom we lean through our pilgrimage, to whom our accents and our deeds are worlds, to whom a word may shoot a pang worse than the stroke of death; surely, I say, if we can do so much for interest, we can do something for goodness and for gratitude. And in all civilized intercourse, how perfectly do we see it ourselves to be the recognized laws of decorum, and if we have not universally good feelings, we have generally, at least, good manners. This may be hypocrisy, but it ought to be sincerity, and we trust it is.

If then we can make our faces to shine on strangers, why darken them on those who should be dear to us! Is it, that we have so squandered our smiles abroad, that we have only frowns to carry home? Is it, that while out in the world, we have been so prodigal of good temper, that we have but our ill humors with which to cloud our firesides? Is it, that it requires often but a mere passing guest to enter, while we are speaking daggers to beings who are nearest to us in life, to change our tone, to give us perfect self-command, that we cannot do for love, what we do for appearance?

Brethren, we can rule our tempers, and we ought. Open the gospel, that most profound philosophy of the human soul, and yet most simple and practical directory of human duty; study it, fill your whole nature with its inspiration; set Christ before you; look upon his calm forehead, his unstormed breast; think how he endured all contradiction of sinners, and endured them to the cross; and on the cross learn of him then, for he was meek and lowly of heart. Think of God, and of the holy peace which is a part of his perfection, and remember that, as we grow into conformity to that, we are more and more his children, and his heirs. Think of Heaven, in which we picture all unity, all goodness, all moral beauty, a tranquil and cloudless light, unpolluted with any malignant, or stormy, or angry passions.

THE GUILT OF CONTEMPT.

Matt. v. 21, 22.

YE HAVE HEARD THAT IT WAS SAID BY THEM OF OLD TIME, THOU SHALT NOT KILL; AND WHOSOEVER SHALL KILL, SHALL BE IN DANGER OF THE JUDGMENT: BUT I SAY UNTO YOU, THAT WHOSOEVER IS ANGRY WITH HIS BROTHER WITHOUT A CAUSE, SHALL BE IN DANGER OF THE JUDGMENT: AND WHOSOEVER SHALL SAY TO HIS BROTHER, RACA, SHALL BE IN DANGER OF THE COUNCIL: BUT WHOSOEVER SHALL SAY, THOU FOOL, SHALL BE IN DANGER OF HELL-FIRE.

In order to take in clearly the spirit of this passage, let us settle in our minds the import of its leading terms. We have here an allusion to three distinct kinds of offence, and to three distinct kinds of penalty. First, " be not angry with your brother without a cause," or you shall be in danger of " the judgment." Secondly, call him not " Raca," or you shall be in danger of " the council." Thirdly, say not unto him " thou fool," or you shall be in danger of " hell-fire " — " the gehenna of fire." Here is a climax of penalty; we infer, therefore, a climax of guilt. The " council " was a subordinate Jewish court. The " judgment " implies a still higher authority. The "gehenna of fire" may be understood from its uses. It means the valley of Hinnom, a place near Jerusalem, were once children had been sacrificed to Moloch, and into which, long afterwards, it was the custom, from the abomination that attached to it, to cast the dead bodies of malefactors. These and other substances needing to be consumed, a fire was incessantly sustained in it; and thence it came to be called the gehenna of fire.

Following the analogy so common in our Lord's — indeed, in all Eastern teaching, by which the spiritual is elicited from the literal — we have an intimation of the order in which these several offences stand by the decision of the holiest and the best. Anger is a passion of resistance; and this unjustly or excessively permitted, is worthy of rebuke. But resistance concedes to an opponent a species of equality. Anger is a passion, therefore, that in some sense implies honor in the object, and does not wholly debase him. It is not, therefore, as guilty as to call him "Raca" — a term of levity and ridicule — which, by robbing its object of the dignity that anger presupposes, merits a still deeper condemnation. But, "Thou fool" — or, as the original more strongly has it, "Thou impious, thou wretch," covers a human being with such odium and such abhorrence, that he who applies the phrase or entertains the spirit of it, subjects himself to the reprobation of outraged humanity and offended Heaven. He strips his brother of all worth, of all nobleness; he excommunicates him from his reverence, from his affections, and takes upon his own head the guilt of a heavy malediction. Anger *may* be sinful; decisive ridicule certainly *is* so. Contempt is the blackest and the worst of all. But the passage involves a contrast as well as a climax: a contrast of the gospel to the law. The law took note of outward transgression; the gospel, of the inward disposition. The law made criminal, injury to man's body, his property, or his name; but the gospel marked, with more solemn indignation, injustice to his soul, the denial of his spiritual claims, the violation of his spiritual rights.

Contempt, contempt of humanity in any form of man, is a great sin. This is the doctrine of Jesus. That man is of worth infinite and ineffable, is the spirit of his teaching, of his practice, of his life; the import of his mission, the significance of his passion and his death: and, therefore, to trample this worth in scorn, is to count the blood of the covenant an unholy thing; to commit one of the darkest offences known in the ethics of the Gospel.

We may trace the guilt of contempt in the evil of its temper. Of course, I do not speak, here, of that sense of unworthiness which we cannot help feeling for what is vile and degrading; I speak of that harsh disposition in which contempt is a habit or a principle. Thus considered, it is evil, and always evil. It cannot, for a moment, clothe itself with the vesture or appearance of an angel. It has the essence of a moral atheism; and of all atheisms this is the worst. If atheism of mere intellect be possible, it does not necessarily exclude some broken aspirations. A speculative atheism is conceivable, which could recognize separate elements of excellence, and separately appreciate them; and though unhappily astray from a Supreme Object, has at least, in chaos, the substance of reverence and devotion. It may have ideals of beauty, of truth, of power, and of goodness; and, while it does not confess the personality of God, unconsciously, it may do honor to his attributes. But so it is not with moral atheism; and, practically, contempt leaves the heart without a God. It wants all the faculties which have affinity with the godlike.

Contempt has no faculty of admiration. It apprehends only inferiority and abasement; and apprehends them only with partiality and falsehood. It is unable to discern honorable and honest qualities visible and distinct, much less the claims of mere humanity when concealed by many obscurations. If, perchance, it *must* look on that which cannot be hidden, and acknowledge that which cannot be denied, it looks with no complacency, and it acknowledges with no affection. Presuming as it does, to spurn others, as unworthy, it is wholly ignorant of that which constitutes the deepest unworthiness. Until we have understood the capacities of a nature, we cannot measure its abuses; until we have fathomed its capability for excellence, we know little of its ruin in transgression. The malignity of sin is revealed only to the soul, when it has comprehended the divinity of goodness. But from such comprehension the spirit of contempt is excluded by the malediction of its own bitterness. Contempt has, therefore, no faculty of reverence. It has no sense of greatness, no sense of beauty; it has no faith in the spiritual, and no trust in the human; it believes not in the immutability of truth, it confides not in the omnipotence of right. It has, of consequence, neither saints nor heroes, neither martyrs nor patriots; but lives unfavored in the seclusion of its own dark and godless being.

A gloomy spirit is this — a spirit misanthropic, a spirit of denial; it has no altar, it has no worship; it has not even the wretched worship of idolatry. In a grand and pure worship, the soul is lifted up, drawn away from self, and absorbed in the glory of its object. It does not so much reflect *on* it, as it exists *in* it; in it lives, moves, and has its being. Hence supreme worship must have its element in the infinite and perfect, and that is, in the one true and only God. That which creates *us*, we worship; but that which *we create*, ourselves, that in which we find ourselves embodied, we idolize. But though idolatry embodies self, yet it is self projected, self taking some outward semblance. The savage carves a piece of wood into the image which his fears have shaped; the Grecian sculptor chisels a piece of marble into a form which the highest fancy has conceived; and both the barbarian and the Greek thus embody a portion of their own being in some independent and outward existence. Contempt does not get even so far as this; but broods over its own chaos, enthroned on its own pride.

Contempt has no faculty of love. It is subversive of all amiable relations; for these relations can only coexist with perceptions of goodness and beauty, and without such perceptions they must perish. Contempt excludes them in every idea we can form of it; it has no such perceptions, and admits no such relations. To hold an object in love and yet contempt, to despise and yet desire, to appreciate and yet scorn, is a contradiction so strange and so absurd, that it could never enter any sane imagination. To the degree, then, that we place our neighbor before us, as an object of contempt, we cut him off from all the best charities of our hearts; we render him an outcast from all the holy offices of fraternity.

As a natural result, this disposition must be fatal to every brotherly sympathy; for, of all antagonisms, scorn is the most repulsive. I do not say, that even scorn may not be melted by the last necessities of want, and that, in extremity, it would stand between a sufferer and the ministries he needed; I do not say, that the most scornful might not pity the forlorn, take the stranger for a season to a home, give the orphan a refuge, and the widow a support; I do not say, that the scornful would weep with no mournful emotion where fire had turned a city to a blackened wilderness, where plague had changed it to a charnel-house, or where earthquake had crumbled it to rubbish; I do not say, that the scornful would not even feed an enemy in his hunger, and give him drink in his thirst; but all this and more, is not enough, if we do not respect a man's nature, and hold the man himself with us in the community of all that entitles that nature to honor.

Contempt, then, is a great sin — contempt of man. It is at variance with the highest principles, and with the highest being; it is at variance with faith, for it sees not the invisible; it is blind in heart to the invisible glory which in every man is enshrined; it is blind in heart to the solemn destiny for which every man is born. It is at variance with hope; it is founded on denial, a denial of capacity in the worst for improvement; a denial of life in the lowest, which may be awakened in a new resurrection; a denial of the worth which lies treasured in every soul, and which, though it may be long tarnished and defaced, may yet have its season of renovation, when it will shine as the stars in glory. It is at variance with charity, which includes both faith and hope, and is their end and their perfection; for charity believeth all things and hopeth all things; and charity is not only pitiful, but reverential, not only most loving, but most humble. It is at variance with God, who despiseth nothing that he has made, and in whose fatherly light all men stand equally as children. It is at variance with humanity, which the Creator made sacred with his likeness, and made immortal with his spirit. It is at variance with Christ, the mediator between God and man, by whom a Father in heaven was revealed, in whom humanity on earth was perfect. In Christ's humanity every man has brotherhood; and in Christ's brotherhood every man has honor. If there be one in our universal race whom the good spirit of Jesus would have scorned or desipsed, then, with impunity, that wretch you may scorn and despise; but, if you can find no such wretch, at your own peril you must venture, and upon your own soul be the consequences.

I have spoken of this ungodly temper, this most un-christ-like disposition, as yet, in its abstract relations. As it exists in actual character, it must, of course, be greatly mixed and modified. But in no single actual character, can it be a permanent or prominent attribute, for such a character would not be human, but diabolical. If asked, however, to specify those, by whom, in ordinary life, it is most commonly manifested, I would answer, — by the pedant in knowledge; by the pharisee in morals; and by the bigot in religion. The pedant is shut up in small delusions, and walks in vain conceits. His path is narrow, and his horizon a speck. He has learned many things which others do not know, but he considers not how many things others know which he has not learned; neither does he consider, that if exchange were made, possibly the gain might be his, and the loss would be theirs. The pedant is one who reads much, and thinks little; has many words, but few ideas: one who does not, like the august and illustrious Newton, compare the discovery which grasped a universe to the finding of a pebble, but rather mistakes the finding of a pebble for the grasping of a universe. This man, insensible to his own insignificance, despises others because he is thus insensible; he is not aware of his own insignificance, and therefore scorns an ignorance, which, perhaps, is only different from his own. Wisdom is tolerant, because it has insight; it has large discourse of reason, because it has much converse with experience; wisdom is humble, because it knows amidst what mysteries it lives — mysteries, that with some scattered stars upon the margin, leave, on all sides of them, a night immeasurable and unfathomable.

The pharisee is to morals, what the pedant is to knowledge; a being of minuteness and formalities. Conformity and not conscience is the essence of his morality; and whatever offends against conformity, whether it be true to conscience, or not, is his highest idea of transgression. The principle or soul of a character, he cannot apprehend; he can only judge whether the outward man walks in the traditions of the elders; and if he does not, it bodes him ill, if the pharisee has power. The pharisee can only read what is set down for him, and he quenches the spirit of God by the letter of the scribes. There is, even in very imperfect characters, much of compensation; but the pharisee can see nothing of this. Evil may be apparent in one direction, while an earnest tendency for good may lie in another; but the pharisee can see nothing of this.

There is also in sin, actual sin, known to be sin, such depths of misery; such ruin, grief, remorse; such haggard wretchedness; such hopeless endurances; that the good man regards it more in sorrow than in anger. The pharisee cannot understand this. There are, too, so many elements of love that often survive through guilt and shame, that the good man, instead of spurning a victim with the voice of judgment, would win him with the call of mercy; and this, least of all, can the pharisee understand. Can you wonder then, that the pharisee did not understand our Saviour? Can you wonder that he was offended with Jesus, who could smile on the outcast; who could eat with those whom the man of long prayers would not touch with the hem of his garment; who could melt the hearts to penitence which this man's scorn had done much to harden; who could tell this man himself, that publicans and harlots would go into the kingdom of heaven before him? It was surely, on the whole, no marvel, that this despiser of the sinful should hate and crucify their Saviour and their Redeemer.

But the darkest of all scorners is the bigot; for, with a presumption in the measure of his contempt, he calls men common or unclean, when they believe otherwise than he believes; and while he takes to himself the seal of salvation, marks them with the brand of perdition. I do not call the man a bigot, who merely supposes another lost in his error, for this may be a conviction which he cannot resist. He may be a man, I admit, of tenderness and mercy; he may hold his opinion with fear and trembling, and look upon his brother whom he regards in the path of ruin, with exceeding sorrow and compassion. But the bigot is not thus. Proud in his assumed humility, elated in his vociferated deprecation, secure in his fancied election, confident as the favorite of grace, his faith becomes actual in a spiritual intolerance, and a practical exclusiveness. He is the one, who says most emphatically to his brother, "Thou fool," "Thou impious," "Thou wretch."

Is this mere supposition? Take knowledge then of the fact, not from the present Church, but from history, and see with what a cruel and sustained malice, this deadly temper could hunt its victims to despair, hoot them with yells of despising hatred, tread them down to vileness, and trample on their prostrate bodies and their prostrate souls. Behold the hapless Jews of the middle ages, the long enduring martyrs of Christian persecution, bigot, contempt and bigotry, scorn; yes, through weary and weary centuries a storm of injury beat on their unsheltered heads, and they have survived, only by bending to it; yes, through weary, weary centuries, insult and ferocity were for the race whom Moses governed, and from whom Jesus sprung.

The guilt of contempt is thus clear in the evil of its temper; the guilt of contempt is no less clear in the evil of its consequences. Contempt lies at the root of all abuses which are most inhuman; it lies at the root of all abuses which have created most misery, of all abuses which have given misery the most lasting power. Contempt of humanity is the most notable cause of wrong to humanity. A blindness to the grandeur that is in man, to the worth of his nature and his soul, is that which generates the hardihood that can behold suffering, or that can enforce it. Insensibility to the worth of man had given up the guilty to cruelty and despair. It was this which wrote laws in blood, and buried persons in darkness; and not until a better spirit prevailed, did mercy change the blood for tears, and raise the persons to the light. As there was no honor, there was no hope; and punishment without benevolence, gratified only the savage instinct to give pain. And so it was with the sinful and other classes—consigned to infamy on which no beam of pity fell, isolated to a cheerless destiny, scorned from sympathy, with no way for amendment or reform, they naturally went from transgression to desperation, and from desperation to impenitence. A light has been taken in our kinder times and by the hand of charity, to guide transgressors into ways of peace. True, the power of Christian love, is yet but feebly trusted, and many most unhappy but not most guilty, are left to perish; still the good Samaritans are gaining in courage, and gaining in number; and with the noiseless steps of evangelical compassion, they seek the secluded paths of the penitent and afflicted; and wherever are the wretched, there they find their mission and find their work.

Insensibility to the worth of man has been the iniquity of rulers, and the source of wrongs innumerable to millions. It has robbed them of their labor; it has taken the sweat of their brow, and not given them bread in their toil; it has chained them to the yoke, and has not shared with them the fruits which they had earned. It placed in every palace a Dives who fared sumptuously, and cared not for the hands that fed him. It placed in every cottage a Lazarus, who contributed to the feast from which he could not even get the crumbs. It has robbed them of their rationality; delivered them to a dire brute ignorance; intercepted all light from their immortal souls, and left them to grope in a dreary bondage-land for any other destiny, than that which appetite might indicate, or which muscle might accomplish. It has robbed them of their lives.

In nothing is insensibility to the worth of man more horribly evident than in disregard to human life. Look at this matter; consider it; see whether it is not so, since the beginning of history. Have not conquerors ever been the same? Have they not always counted men as they counted clods, and estimated the relations of vital forces with as little thought of misery or happiness as if these forces had been mechanical and not mortal? Had such thought operated, surely humanity would have been spared a thousand wars which have cursed it; and millions who have been marched to the slaughter of hellish conflict, by insane ambition, would have closed their eyes in peace, with benison and prayer. But these multitudes of the lowly had no reverence before kings: they were simply a certain quantity of motive power of disposable physical energy, to be directed as their masters' will impelled; mere instruments to be used or broken, as their master's pleasure required. Insensibility to the worth of man is at the bottom of all Slaveries — white Slaveries or black.

The essence of tyranny is contempt: this is its origin, and this its perpetuation. Woman is the first in the order of captives, for the savage despises weakness; and the husband-savage, who coerces and yet insults his wife, is the first master in a house of bondage.

And woman continues to be a slave, whether as drudge to her savage lord, or delight to her civilized superior, until her spiritual worth is apprehended, her moral dignity acknowledged, and her liberty recognized in the glory of the soul. Contempt, I repeat, is the essence of tyranny : it is the spirit of oppression ; it is the most deadly foe to freedom. It is a chain for the slave, stronger than all the manacles which were ever forged ; it is worse than bandages of iron seventy times enfolded ; it fixes generations after generations where the stern allotments of caste have placed them ; it would render degradation an eternal and a changeless fate. It fastens the serf to the soil of his lord, and by the will of that lord the space is determined, in which he has leave to toil and leave to live. Yea, yet more than this combined with rapacity, it has torn the poor barbarian from his native earth, from every instinctive affection and every human privilege ; it has crammed him in a wooden hell ; and if life could stand the tug of torture, borne him to his doom through the wild roar of waters. There is a pathway paved with bones across the broad Atlantic ; and every fathom beneath is a black man's sepulchre, and every wave above has been his winding sheet. Oh, if the ocean could give up its dead ! Oh, if these bones could live ! a cloud of witnesses against the iniquity of Christendom would gather from the caverns of the deep, to affright the earth, to appal and overshadow the heavens!

Who will say, that contempt had no part in this terrific wrong? Who will say, that contempt did nothing to perpetuate the bondage which this terrific wrong commenced. We know that the uncivilized heart is cruel to what is strange, and cruel from contempt. It despises a difference of manners, or of person; and it compares *all* disadvantageously with itself. But rapacity can render the unsanctified heart as cruel as the uncivilized; and *this*, the sufferings of unhappy and unprotected millions all over the sinful world, can testify with groanings which cannot be uttered! Contempt — stern, heartless, and godless — in every place of this sinful earth where man causes grief to man in permanent injustice — yes, in every such afflicted place, contempt lives and rules. Wherever the weak, the poor, the ignorant, the lowly, are alienated and wronged, there contempt is present and predominant. Said I not well, then, that contempt is a great sin — a sin which has its testimonies in all the testimonies of oppression, in the sighs of unrewarded toil, in the degradation of working masses, in the power of stern aristocracies, in the carnages of war, in miseries and slaveries almost as old as the world, and as wide.

The spirit of contempt is the true spirit of Antichrist,

for no other is more directly opposed to Christ. When Jesus entered on his ministry, it was the master passion of the times, whether in the haughty Roman or the scornful Jew; in the Roman, proud; and in the Jew, austere. Against Jesus, this temper came in deadly conflict; and from none was the opposition fiercer than from his own countrymen. In one form or another, the temper pervaded Jewish life. It sat in the chair of the scribe; it presided on the tribunal of the judge; it walked in the market-place; it took the chief rooms at feasts; it claimed the highest seats in the synagogues; and it prayed with lofty looks in the temple. Our Lord scouted this ungodliness with a holy opposition. He met it by the inculcation of a humble and a loving spirit; by the revelation of a heavenly dignity in humanity, which rebuked scornful assumption as both mean and blasphemous. And then to words, such as men had never heard, he added an example such as men had never seen. He went himself among the outcast; he took his part with the despised; he sojourned among the scorned; he was to be found mixed with the vulgar multitude; he was to be met in poor men's homes and at poor men's meals. The publican whom the pharisee spurned, received from Jesus no rebuke; the sinner and Samaritan addressed him as their friend; and those whom all had given to reprobation, whom the world had marked with ineffable infamy, came to Jesus, attracted by the grace that was around him, and took from his lips the words of forgiveness, and the assurance of peace.

And that his example might in all things be complete, his ministry ended as it had begun. He came not to call the righteous, but sinners to repentance; and as in life he did not shun the wretched, he was numbered with the transgressors in his death. Contumely, hatred, insult, collected together to hoot him from existence, until nailed upon the cross — the instrument of vile and ignominious torture — between two thieves, he gave up the ghost. The spirit of that life, the spirit of that death, yet maintained the contest; and the contest will not end, until this fated temper is subdued; until every man has due honor, as a child of God, and a brother of Jesus; until every man feels in himself, and recognizes in his fellow the divinity of an immortal soul, and the dignity of everlasting relations. Not until right is founded on reverence, will it be secure; not until duty is based upon love, will it be complete; not until liberty is based upon eternal principles, will it be full, equal, lofty, and universal. Then, and only then, will the mind of Christ have entered into the heart of the millions, who, as yet, have but his name upon their lips; then will his true kingdom have enlarged its bounds and increased its glory; then shall his sceptre have sway, and his throne be established in justice, in virtue, and in freedom.

Oh, that each of us had the hallowed spirit of our divine master abiding within us! He, who had the wealth of heaven, despised no poverty. He, who had the wisdom of God, companioned with the ignorant and the rude. He, who was without blemish and without spot, — whom no man could accuse of sin, — with whom Jehovah, the righteous and the holy, was well pleased, — did not scorn the sinful; he did pity them. O man, whosoever thou art, that trustest in thyself and despisest others; O man, whosoever thou art, that lookest on thy brother with social or with spiritual contempt; O man, whosoever thou art, that sayest to thy brother, even in the whisperings of thy thought, "Thou fool, stand aside, for I am nobler, I am wiser, I am holier than thou,"— turn to the face of God's anointed and be covered with repentant shame; turn to the face of God's anointed, be of converted heart, and do this evil thing no more, no more forever.

EVANGELICAL GOODNESS.

MARK xii. 41–44.

AND JESUS SAT OVER AGAINST THE TREASURY, AND BEHELD HOW THE PEOPLE CAST MONEY INTO THE TREASURY: AND MANY THAT WERE RICH CAST IN MUCH; AND THERE CAME A POOR WIDOW, AND SHE THREW IN TWO MITES, WHICH MAKE A FARTHING. AND HE CALLED UNTO HIM HIS DISCIPLES, AND SAITH UNTO THEM, VERILY I SAY UNTO YOU, THIS POOR WIDOW HATH CAST IN MORE THAN ALL THEY WHICH HAVE CAST INTO THE TREASURY. FOR ALL THEY DID CAST IN OF THEIR ABUNDANCE: BUT SHE OF HER WANT DID CAST IN ALL THAT SHE HAD, EVEN ALL HER LIVING.

THE scene described in this passage is most impressive and affecting when we contemplate it from the position of our Saviour. Much there is of solemn beauty in the mere situation and the surrounding view, but this becomes tragic and sublime when connected with its spiritual associations. Before, was the temple with all its national memories, and all its suggested sanctity; its majesty unbent, and its loveliness unsoiled; but ere a few years should roll along, its glory would be scattered in the dust. Jerusalem was then a city of life and action, but the time was coming, was near at hand, when desolations would be in her streets, and solitude in her palaces. The Roman eagle, it is true, had already flapped above her with his blood-stained wings; the Roman arm had already crushed her independence, still there was something of the past, in which the children of Zion might exult. A voice from the Sanctuary told what they once had been; the cloud of former greatness still lay upon existing monuments; the spirits of patriarchs and prophets addressed them from the tombs; and while the temple raised its towers in their sight, one grand object, at least remained, around which they could assemble with delight, and on which they could gaze without a blush.

While our Saviour overlooked this scene, and saw with sad concern the immediate future big with destruction, and ready to engulf it, it is no irreverence against him, to suppose, that he thought not unmoved of his own sufferings, which were soon to take place here,—sufferings to which more than once he had vaguely pointed, but of which lately he had plainly spoken. It is no irreverence against him to suppose, that he saw, not without shrinking, the cup of sorrow drawing towards him with invisible approaches, and which would quickly be at his lips; that he saw not, without revulsion, the passion of many agonies that awaited him, with the cross of shame and torture rising up in the midst of them; and it is not irreverence against, but affection for him, to suppose, that grief lay the more heavily on his soul, by the knowledge that such things must come upon him in the city of his kindred, at the hands of brethren, whom to the last he loved; whom he would so often have gathered together to shield from the destroyer, even as a hen gathereth her chickens under her wings.

Our Saviour mused and was silent. Numbers were collecting to the treasury of the temple, and passing away again. Many conspicuous personages, doubtless, were among the crowd. The zealous pharisee would be there; and the learned scribe, and the reigning demagogue, and the popular doctor, and the eloquent orator; there would be the priest, to whom the temple was dear as witness to the authority of his order; there would be the patriot, to whom the temple was not less dear as witness to the glory of his country. Our Saviour specifies no one of these; he allowed them to pass on; he left them to obscurity. He mused, and still was silent. The temple with all its garniture, moulders in the ashes of centuries; the names of those who were the most noted in assemblies are buried in its silence; but the whole of them lie in the deep of the Past, and no epitaph exists above them, to mark their grave. Our Saviour mused, and was silent; but as he mused, a widow came, and cast in two mites that made a farthing, and her's was the offering which our Saviour noted. He perceived in it the inward goodness of an upright soul; he gave it the value of his perfect sanction, and, wherever the Gospel shall be preached, it shall be known for a memorial and an example.

The memorial is familiar. All who have heard or read the words of the evangelical story, have the widow and her mite among the most vivid of their religious thoughts. The lesson which the example teaches is as obvious as the record of it is familiar. The record is often recited, and the lesson is often enforced, yet the frequency is not greater than it is needed. It is for our constant good to return again and again to the examples in which our Saviour embodies his principles, by which he illustrates his teachings. They are never exhausted, and there is no time when we cannot draw from them instruction and refreshment. Besides, if we are at all earnest for improvement, we require them for light and for guidance; we require them for security and correction. There is much to set us wrong within us; there is much to set us wrong outside. Sophistry gets easily into our reasonings when we seek for conclusions favorable to our inclinations, and for such conclusions we are often on the search. Our motives are not unfrequently unsound when we would flatter ourselves that they are honest. Our vanities and passions can mask themselves in infinite disguises, assume those which our self-love would have them. We would have self-indulgence, yet not lose self-respect; and, to make the compromise effectual, we compact most artificial and elaborate systems of self-deception. The world in which we live sustains and aids us in this bad exertion. Fashion, pretension, expediency, convention, custom, tradition, all the thousand conspiracies to veil the hatefulness of evil; to obscure the true nature of sin; to evade the solemn injunctions of moral obligation, yet escape dishonor by extended participation; to put aside reality and to substitute appearance; to put good for evil, and evil for good; — all these tendencies fall in with the predispositions of our own hearts, and our own hearts are fatally ready to make alliance with them. But the subterfuges are shamed by the teaching of Christ, and like the demons of old, if not always cast out, they are rebuked to silence in his presence. When, however, we sincerely look for wisdom, he is always near to us in his word, and with that we can cut asunder the most knotted web-work which sophistry ever put together.

The principle in the example before us, as in all the evangelical illustrations, is manifest; in each, the narrative at once reveals the thought contained in it. In this, the idea obviously is, that genuine goodness is in the inward soul, and not in the outward action; that the intention gives value to the deed; that the measure of excellence is not the amount of the gift, but the amount of purity in giving, and the amount of sacrifice that is made to give. One may give much and it may cost him little; another may give little, and it may cost him all.

On the abstract principle I will say no more; genuine goodness belongs to the soul, and action is of merit in the agent, is a portion of noble character, only as it is the fruit of rectitude within. I will point out a few characteristics of evangelical goodness.

Evangelical goodness is unostentatious. How pure and beautiful is the goodness of this widow in Israel. We can almost paint her to our fancies, as she shrinks stealthily through the crowd, to cast her unnoticed mite into the treasury of her country and her God; then drawing aside the veil which shrouds the eternal world, we behold this lowly child of earth honored of that equal Father by whom goodness in the most secret thought is loved, and in the smallest deed rewarded. Our Lord constantly insists on this quality of the worth that gains acceptance at the supreme tribunal. "When ye fast," he says, "be not of a sad countenance, that ye appear not unto men to fast. When you pray, enter into your closet, shut the door, and pray to your Father, who seeth in secret. When you give alms, do not sound the trumpet before you, as the hypocrites do." This surely does not preclude from moral excellence every open manifestation; for such would not be possible without destroying, at the same time, a great mass of the virtue which adorns human character, and which blesses the world. Our Lord would not surely forbid all public humiliation, or any fasting, but that which God alone should know. He would not surely forbid all social prayer, and all common worship. He would not surely forbid all demonstrative benevolence, all associative charities. Doctrine to this effect would not only reduce human beings to isolated individuals, and leave no place for the existence of example, — it would contradict other teachings of our Lord himself; for he says, "Let your light so shine before men that they may see your good works, and glorify your Father who is in heaven." Such a doctrine would have deprived the world of his own example; for were nothing perfect but what is secret, then he had in his holiness remained invisible forever. Such a doctrine is, then, contradictory not only to his teaching, — it is equally contradictory to his practice. He fasted with the knowledge of his disciples. He prayed in their presence. He attended worship in the synagogues, and in the temple. And with multitudes for witnesses he performed miracles of beneficence.

It is to the *spirit* of a character that our Lord's remarks apply. The character that he loved was one that had vitality which was not nourished from without, but which had the supply of its power from within; which adhered to the just or the good, simply because it was just or good; which shunned publicity, whenever publicity could be avoided or was needless; which, having joy in the sight of heaven, cared not for the praise of men, and, indifferent to their neglect, could even bear with their contempt. Our Lord would drive no man to a solitary asceticism, which has often more of ostentation than all the vanities of life. On the contrary, he required of his most immediate disciples to go forth fearlessly into throngs; to enter boldly into the cities of Israel and the gentiles; yet did he rebuke down every impulse that seemed officious or obtrusive. He himself toiled openly on the highways and in the market-places, nor did he refuse to be a guest with rulers and the wealthy; but those to whom he most frequently resorted, those with whom he held most intimate and most friendly communion, were a quiet family in Bethany, embosomed in the sacredness of noiseless virtue.

We cannot always calculate the influence of others upon us; and without any positive insincerity, much that we do and say, much that we leave undone and unsaid, is attributable to such influence. Evils may be in our conduct, and go on unchecked, so long as they do not disturb the system in which we live, so long as they provoke no censure from those who form the circle in which we move. We try them by no moral standard that is independent on conventional opinions; and until we perceive their deformity revealed by the avoidance or the frowns of society, we scarcely know them to be evils. In like manner, we perform actions of seeming virtue, without discovering, for a time, how much of the virtue is no more than seeming. We have no purpose to deceive, and yet, unconsciously, many of our actions have being because a multitude of witnesses behold them. These actions would not have being if witnesses were not; but of this fact we would ourselves be ignorant. It is thus that others become to us sometimes a conscience, and sometimes a delusion; but more frequently a delusion than a conscience.

There are actions, to be sure, of singleness and worth, that cannot escape from the world's applause, and to which the applause that the world gives is true, heart-felt, and permanent. But the souls, to whom such actions are native, wonder at the praise which comes to them, and they are mortified by the notoriety that follows. If they have risked their lives, and been the means of saving others, — if, in severe distress, they have shared a small relief with some whose situation was worse than theirs and had no relief whatever, — they are surprised and humbled to find that deeds so natural should have praise so exaggerated. The exaggeration springs from this, that human nature cannot help admiring generosity, and but few men are really generous. When, however, the actions have all the marks of a genuine heroism, we can pardon the exaggeration, and we can regard with leniency the contrast between men's actual deeds and the ideal of their nature out of which the exaggeration comes.

But there are other forms of it, which are not to be so regarded, because they evince a low standard of action, and tend to keep it low, if not to render it lower. Take one or two familiar cases. A man of station, president or prince, listens patiently to a story of distress, and perhaps bestows a kindness on the teller of it; possibly, in his walks, he discovers a beggar that has fainted on the way, and he helps him to arise, and supports him to a shelter; — actions, charitable, it is admitted, but extremely simple, and which, if done by a plain private man, would arouse no special commendation in the smallest village ; but as it was a prince or president that did it, Panegyric puffs at the trumpet of fame almost to suffocation, to let the world be aware of what prince and president can do to prove that they belong to the family of men. Now, in the circumstances, what else could prince or president have done? Could he, if he had a heart, have stifled the words of the unfortunate, or have left a fellow-creature without aid to perish? What did he more than others? And to say, that without infamy he might have done less, would be to hold forth a wretched view of the character of the individual, or of the influence of his position ; it would be to libel humanity, or to malign the man.

Again : a person, worth hundreds of thousands, dispenses a portion of it in public improvement and general charities. He bestows five thousand upon one object, ten thousand upon another; and he does this more than once. If he be really a good man, he *does* venture on a martyrdom ; for I can hardly think of a severer persecution to be endured by a modest and humane nature, than to have his name emblazoned in the journals as *his* will be. If he has chosen wisely, he has acted well; but he intended good, at any rate, and intention in such case is virtue. "But what," he asks himself, "ought I to have done? If many rich men would not have done so, it does not exalt my virtue ; it merely exhibits their sordidness; it shows to what an extent mean ideas prevail upon the purposes and use of wealth. What can I do with my wealth but distribute it? This will be done, whether I do it or not; and, it is likely, to worse ends. I ought not to leave it all to my family; I would not spend it all on myself, and I could not if I would. My possessions abound and overflow beyond every desire, not merely of need, but of luxury; what is more simple, more easy, what less a sacrifice, and more a gratification, than to benefit my generation out of these ample stores?"

"What," said a plain man, of no wonderful fortune, who had given a thousand pounds to a single charity school, — and this was but one gift out of many to such purposes, — "what," said he, at a public meeting where he had to bear a martyrdom of eulogy, "what have I done, but given a pound apiece to a thousand poor children?" Little did he understand of oratory; but a true elevation of soul, an honest simplicity of heart, made him sublimely eloquent. But, though it is mortifying to our nature, we must confess, that the world's fulsome praise is the expected exchange for many a largess. Appeals are constantly made not only to men's vanity, but even to their senses, — ay, and to their appetites; their subscriptions are won from them by the paragraph in the newspaper, or by the gaud of the showy fair, or by the viands of the luxurious feast.

Was it to teach us virtue in its own sweet beauty, that our Lord shows it to us ever in situations where we cannot suspect it to be under the dominion of influences such as these? Was it to show it to us delivered from all delusive associations, from all connection with motives of interest or fascinations of the senses, that he places it invariably before us in positions unnoticed and obscure? Our Lord, in his teachings, did not adduce what we call illustrious examples. The models of excellence which he selects are never distinguished by any outward celebrity. It was not such that mankind needed, nor was it such that our Saviour could have used. Striking and brilliant characters are abundant in all the histories of earth. It was his mission to teach us that characters might have a nobler elevation than these, and yet be neither striking nor brilliant. We required to be instructed in the holy as well as the heroic; in the devoted sense of right which can be magnanimous without fame, — which may shine on the lowly paths of life even more brightly than on its highways, — which may be as exalted in the closet-prayer, or in the secret alms, as in the hour of martyrdom.

And this is the instruction which he has given us in every mode by which the soul can be reached; — by precept, by example, by allegory, and by fact. When we enter into the spirit of these instructions, we learn how little we know of life when we see it only in its outside appearance. What can we know of the mystery of lives that pass around us? What can we know of the unexplored, unspoken, and unspeakable things which lie deep in the secrecies of these immortal beings? We know little of their evil, and less still of their goodness. The most eloquent language in which truest admiration ever spoke its sense of a blessed and benignant man, is infantile stammering to those who lived in the sunshine of his presence; yet, even to them, there were mysteries of inward holiness to which they had never pierced. We see not all of moral beauty in its external and accidental attributes. Its purest loveliness is not often where the many would be allowed to gaze, or where they would be fit to judge. We catch but glimpses of the best life; we see it only in a few prominent aspects, as we behold not all of God's bountiful earth in its peopled spaces. There are wonders of God upon the earth in yet unbroken loneliness; things which the eye hath not seen, nor the ear heard, lavished in the very profusion of unbounded power, in the exhaustless abundance and wealth of omnipotence. There are floods of sunshine flung over the broad sweep of untrodden deserts; gorgeous foliage and eternal bloom clothing the wilderness of virgin woods. There are rivers that wander over voiceless regions; there are beautiful, but unnoted shores, washed only by the ocean wave, cheered only by the music of the storm. There are spots of Paradise lovely in their solitude, which the day-beams and the moon-light alone look upon. There are unprofaned cataracts, by which Nature, in her deep retreats, hymns forever her anthems of lonely praise. And so it is with the good man's soul: it has glory in its secret places; it has joy in its hidden depths; it has light where no man intrudes; it has peace which passeth understanding and passeth utterance; it has majesty and bliss, where only its own thought with the spirit of its God reposes.

Evangelical goodness is self-forgetful and self-denying. It does not render the individual a centre, drawing to himself advantages from all around; but rather a centre from which advantages to others emanate and flow. The ruling sentiment in a loving and a godly heart is to increase the sum of pure enjoyment in the world, to diminish the quantity of pain there; to add force to the efforts of virtue, and to weaken the power of sin; to do this without thinking aught of its own indulgence, and to do it even at the cost of much endurance and much opposition. This is more than amiable instinct. It is more than the instinct of affection;

it is more than to reverence our parents or to cherish our offspring. It is more than the instinct of gratitude; it is more than to aid those who have aided us, and to bless those who love us. It is to work for a stranger; it is to suffer for an enemy. The goodness which proves the endeavor for a high moral and spiritual life, is more than prudence. It is more than general propriety of conduct, modesty of speech, honesty of dealing, and temperance of habits. Inward rectitude will, of course, issue in these, but will not stop in them. Worldly wisdom, even outward necessity, will compel men thus far, or crush them if they refuse to move. Nor does character evince any purer tone, if it is merely acted on by the hope of future happiness and the fear of future misery; for it is only carrying the selfish hopes and fears of *this* world to another. Up to this point, then, we stand on no elevated height in the region of virtue, if we even can be said to have entered it.

Suppose a life, and let it be above the average; take away from it the kindness which belongs to its natural affections, the amenities that pertain to friendship, the benefits which it has conferred from gratitude or expectation; take away from it the order which social restraint or social obligation has enforced. Leave with it its adherence, in every other respect, to personal inclination, its devotion to individual passions, its violations of charity, without remorse, both in temper and in speech; leave with it its concealments and emulations, its excuses and its subterfuges; leave with it its indifference to the great concerns of humanity, and its quick sensibility to the little concerns of itself; leave with it its apathy to enormous wrong which does not press too nearly, its more than tolerance if it promises or gives emolument; leave with it the sophistry with which it can obscure an everlasting truth, and the logic with which it can sustain to itself an everlasting lie, when the truth calls for sacrifice and the lie is favorable to indulgence; in short, give it credit for the tithe of mint, anise, and cummin, but charge on it neglect in the weightier matters of the law, judgment, mercy, and faith: what portion of it remains to be esteemed as genuine, as Christian virtue? No, this is more than instinct, than prudence, than propriety; it is the practice of excellence in its changeless right; it is the love of it in its eternal fairness. To this belongs an integrity which is higher than the world, and which nothing in the world can move; an integrity which fears only to sin, to which all things spiritually great are possible; for with such integrity there is ever connected a mighty zeal, — a zeal which keeps alive that holy fire in the soul, which inflames but does not consume, — the zeal which makes enthusiasm god-like, which endows the will with a moral omnipotence, which clothes the spirit with glory and arms the tongue with lightning.

Christian goodness is not only a spirit of purity; it is also a spirit of sacrifice. And to exercise the spirit of sacrifice in its utmost devotion, we need not the trials of fiery persecution. Life does not permit that such can be frequent, and even in the fiercest times such can be only transient and rapid. The opportunity is rare, which concentrates the sanctity of a whole nature in a single resolve; but the opportunities are always, when a sanctity as pure can leaven the entire life, and be the principle that animates its every action. For the existence or energy of such a spirit, the torture or the stake is no essential. *We* are not called to answer for our faith before magistrates. *We* are not appointed to make confession in the flames. *We* are ordained to duties which meet us every day, which with every day impose on us self-denial, in which every day we may consecrate endurance by tempers both heavenly and heroic. We have bereavements that sadden us; we have vexations that provoke us; we have labors that oppress, and watchings that fatigue; we have losses and griefs which it requires believing hearts to support. Now, we may bear all these meekly, and that is to bear them nobly, to perfect the dictates of celestial wisdom in the strength of a sublime patience. This may be without conspicuous position and without emblazoned story. The daily sacrifices of a laboring man to duty may involve more bravery of soul than the achievements of patriots and heroes; and the devotion of an unlettered girl, comforting through years the bed-ridden winter of a parent's age, may contain a holier martyrdom than any which the church has canonized and glorified. The spirit of sacrifice is preëminently the spirit of Christ; it is the spirit which was perfect on the cross, and which gave the cross its triumph.

Evangelical goodness is elevated, broad, generous, liberal. The widow devoted her offering to the temple, and the temple was the outward symbol to her of her God and of her brethren. The widow found the embodiment of her holiest ideas in the temple of Jerusalem. But the Christian finds the incarnation of *his* in the living heart of Jesus; that heart which felt for all that struggled in the flesh, yet breathed itself in the invisible and the infinite; that heart which was perfect in its love, which went up without a stain to the Father in heaven, and went out without a limit to all his children upon earth; that heart which adored the Creator in all the compass of his attributes, and sympathized with man in all the extent of his wants.

While the widow presented her offering to the temple of Jerusalem, there was planned a greater temple, of which she did not know. It was even then being founded; ample were to be its mansions and beautiful its courts, Jesus to be its priest, and all nations its worshippers. In the death-sigh that tore the sacred breast of Jesus, the partition walls of a thousand divisions were overturned ; to the tribes of every tongue and clime and color, a common kindred was proclaimed; and that veil which was rent asunder in the old temple was never to be restored in the new.

This new temple is spiritual, a building not made with hands, dedicated to the highest glory of God, for the best happiness of man. To this temple *we* are called to contribute, and each of us may give his portion; one of his abundance, another of his poverty, and yet each be the richer for what he gives. Here is space enough for every talent and every effort. Much is to be done, and all may be done in peace. The first temple was erected without sound of hammer or use of iron instrument; still more must this later and holier be raised without the sounds of unrighteous strife and of carnal warfare. The materials of the first temple were made ready in solitude. Those of the last also must be shaped in retirement; in the silence of the heart; in the quietness of home; in the practice of unostentatious duty. And there is not a single act of goodness, nor a pure desire, nor a sincere aspiration after truth; not a soul enlightened by religion, not an intellect delivered from ignorance; not a bosom cleared of passion; not a conscience strengthened against sin, — in which a stone is not polished or a gem brightened for this most sacred structure. In this good work all is harmony; nothing of right endeavor is useless, and nothing of the humblest work is lost. The teacher that enlightens an infant contributes to it as well as the prophet that instructs a world; and both are fellow-workers with Christ, both are fellow-workers with God. In this good work all degrees and all modes of generous action are united; and whatever differences may otherwise separate the agents, in this they have unbroken and sublime communion, — in this they are gloriously joined together in the holy alliance of human brotherhood, in the sacred compact of universal virtue.

THE SPIRIT OF CHRISTIAN FORGIVENESS.

LUKE vi. 37.

FORGIVE, AND YE SHALL BE FORGIVEN.

MY object in this discourse is to make some general remarks on the spirit of mutual forgiveness, as inculcated in the religion of Christ.

But, before entering directly on my subject, I wish to state a few preliminary reflections. And, first, as to the nature of the doctrine. It is not one, evidently, of untaught instinct. We scarcely ever hear of it in the savage, with whom it is equally a duty to inflict vengeance without mercy, and a glory to bear it without complaint. Neither is it one of imperfect conditions of society, or of incomplete revelation. It was not a part of heathen teaching, nor is it conspicuous in the Jewish Scriptures. It was but little heard in the Gentile schools; and whatever had been originally intended by the Jewish Legislator, in the maxim "An eye for an eye, and a tooth for a tooth," it is sufficiently evident, that the maxim was afterwards so used as to justify the most vindictive malice. The doctrine of forgiveness, in its full breadth and beauty, is of Christ and of Christianity. Christianity founds it on that most affectionate of all relations, the relation that subsists between children and a parent; and such is the relation which it reveals as between humanity and God. We are his weak and feeble offspring; if we turn towards him, he is ever ready to look upon us with mercy and compassion; he knoweth that we are but dust, and he pitieth us, even as a father pitieth his children. And thus benignly lovely in its principle, it is no less lovely in its example. Christ it was who taught it; and with what sweet and varied eloquence did he teach it! Read the precepts in which he commands it; the motives by which he urges it; the sanctions by which he enforces it; the stories and the parables by which he illustrates it; and, if these do not show you how divinely fair it is, you have no sympathy with the soul of moral beauty. Yet this word, sublimely as it was uttered, was only the breathing of a life, which was the substance and the perfection of that sentiment which the word contained.

Secondly, as to the limits of the doctrine. Although it refers to evil done by others against us, — evil which wounds our feelings or our interests, — it does not require us to see even that evil otherwise than it is; for, if it did, it would do us the deepest injury: it would require of us to blind both our intellect and conscience; and worse than this no enemy could inflict upon us. It tasks us with no such impossibility; it would have us look at sin exactly as it is, if so we can apprehend it; and it would mitigate no righteous judgment which, in justice, we can pronounce against it. Still it would shield from our hatred the *person* of the sinner. Nor does it exact indifference to the evils which are done us, or affection to those who do them; it would simply repress feelings of vindictiveness, and control the will against movements and actions of enmity. We are called on to discourage those irritating feelings, not to add to them or excite them; not to inflame wrong by dwelling on it; and not to make our own tempers the advocates of our own cause. Who, more than Christ, ever abhorred sin? who more alive to its iniquity? who more sublimely, more terribly uncompromising in denouncing it? yet who, at the same time, more gentle, more merciful? Who more keen, more sensitive, more delicate than he in his feelings, and whoever had his feelings so grossly wounded? Yet was there no shadow of return or revenge! Indeed, there is something to me fearful in the manner in which a good man deals with sin and sinners. From angry rebuke I would not shrink; violent denunciation I should not value; but the calm decision of a holy and gentle mind, unmovedby temper or by self, is to me the most awful thing in the universe, except the disapprobation of the all-seeing Creator himself. There was, therefore, neither weakness nor blindness in the doctrine of forgiveness as Christ taught and as Christ practised it.

And, thirdly, a word as to the reason why this noble doctrine has not more effect among professing Christians. A strong reason, no doubt, can be found in our individual and our emulative desires; but another — and it is the only one which I will glance at — exists in the powers which social prejudices have upon us. As these prejudices spring out of the individual nature, so they react back again upon it, and increase the evils in it from which they spring. One of the most obstinate of these prejudices is the glory which has as yet been associated with physical combat. Success, victory, overpowers the imagination of the mass; and as the imagination of the mass is mainly acted on through the senses, the victory which most affects them is victory obtained in external strife. Our religion was ushered in by songs of angels, and these songs were of peace; and yet never, since earth drank the first human blood, have there been fiercer warriors than the professors of this religion. Our religion was incarnate in one whose voice was not heard in the streets; but never have yells of slaughter more wrathfully torn the sky than the yells which those who call themselves by his name have shouted or provoked. The banner of our faith is the symbol of endurance; and the last words of *Him* who died upon this cross, in which we profess to glory, were words of pardon; but that kind of spirit is one which most Christians since would not have honored, but scorned. Christ expired in a space which was "called the field of blood," and his followers have made, that field almost as broad as the earth; more earnestly have they imbibed the passions of the Roman soldiers than the meek spirit of the crucified, who hung in agony amidst their lances. While these incongruities exist in our religious sentiment, it is not likely that our individual or social morality can be very harmonious or consistent. Yet, however we may fail in practice, it is well at least not to lower the standard of our duty; and this of forgiveness is not the less excellent or the less obligatory, because all and each of us constantly transgress it.

I. I will proceed now to notice some qualities which distinguish the spirit of Christian forgiveness.

1. It is comprehensive. It teaches us to see a *brother* even in our enemy; for our enemy is a *man;* and though he excludes us from his benevolent re-

gards, it is not for us to exclude him from ours. Enmity does not justify the return of enmity. Injury is no plea for injury. To return passion for passion is the instinct of resistance; to return good for good is the instinct of sympathy; and though the latter is the impulse of complacency, it is no more a moral principle than the former: it is still an instinct. To be pleased with those who admire us, is surely not an effort; to bear with the incidental inconsistencies of those who permanently esteem us, is confessedly no martyrdom. "If you salute your brethren only," says our Saviour, "what do ye more than others? But I say unto you, love your enemies; also, do good to those that hate you; bless those that curse you, and pray for those that calumniate and despitefully use you." The spirit, therefore, of Christian forgiveness, or even Christian forbearance, is something superior to the instinct of sympathy, and it is yet more than a triumph over the instinct of resistance. It is a wise and calm benevolence, founded on belief in God, and on brotherhood with man, strengthened by our love to Christ; and, thus founded, it rests upon a basis which passion cannot shake, and rises to an open clearness of elevation which prejudice cannot darken. The case does not exist, and never has existed, for which the gospel allows no mercy; and the gospel is the Christian's rule. It is the rule we acknowledge, and it is the rule we should practise; for it came from the mind of God, and was made living in the heart of Christ.

2. The spirit of Christian forgiveness is inward and simple. It is "from the heart" that Jesus requires that his disciples should forgive men their trespasses; and the forgiveness which comes not from the heart is but a mockery and a name. It must be ample, cordial, frank, cheerful, and unreserved. For the want of this simplicity, many reconciliations are but outward, and, therefore, are unsound. Men still retain corroding ideas, jealousies, and want of confidence. Littleness comes in contact with littleness. A small passion in one has strife with a like small passion in another; vanity with vanity, cunning with cunning, covetousness with covetousness, ambition with ambition; and the struggle is all the more inveterate, if both are of contracted minds. Their battle is on the earth; their hearts are of the earth; the objects which they strive after belong to earth; but the fire which keeps alive the contest is fire from hell.

A great difficulty, even to the beginning of reconciliation, exists in pride. It often happens that two persons, who greatly esteem each other, fall out concerning a trifle. Pride holds them silent, and silence deepens their alienation, until, at last, two minds, which had once been linked together in the closest regard, have a gulf fixed between them, dark, fathomless, and impassable. It sometimes also occurs, that one arrives at the conviction that he has painfully wounded the feelings of another, that he has offended him, that he has done him injustice; but here again pride closes his mouth, and, sooner than make a candid acknowledgment, he is content to endure the torture of a sense of guilt. Or it may be that he *fears* the person whom he has offended, and dares not venture to ask him for pardon, lest he should find only repulsion and refusal. O the supreme excellence, on this point, that appears in the character of Christ! Was there ever a penitent who dreaded to approach him? Is it that the pure only can afford to forgive? Is it that they who have evils of their own feel called on to evince a stronger detestation against the infirmities of others? Is it that they consider this a restitution for former transgressions, and a peace-offering to insulted virtue? He is either a very pure man, or a very blind man, whose conscience has nothing wherewith to upbraid him; but, in being hasty to fling the first stone at his brother, he would give more evidence of blindness than of purity. But some men cannot forgive graciously. They would have the offender stand before them with bare feet and with uncovered head, until they had exacted the uttermost farthing of humiliation. They inflict full penance, and, after all, give but half an absolution. Thus the first step to kindness is prevented; for most men would rather be hated than humiliated. The pardon which blunts the sense of dignity is better withheld than given, and better dispensed with than sought for. Now, my brethren, granting that we have had most irritating cause for anger, yet, if we discover that the object of our anger grieves most sincerely for his fault, would deprecate our resentment and conciliate our peace, if still we hold sternly to our severity, our feeling is then, not anger, but malice,—not indignation, but revenge. We are then the farthest possible from the mind of Christ; we are then the farthest possible from the mind of God.

Both in his manner of teaching forgiveness, and in his manner of bestowing it, Christ manifests a tender regard for the rights of a human being; and most beautifully does he show how an offender may be pardoned without being degraded. His instruction and his example impart and manifest the same truth, and that is, the heavenly excellence of a generous clemency. There was no remonstrance in the tones of that father who wept on the neck of his recovered son; and there was no sharpness in that look which shot conviction to the heart of Peter. But the spirit of Christian forgiveness rises immeasurably higher than this. It is not simply meek to repentance, it is superior to provocation; it is not simply placable in triumph, it is merciful in agony; it has not merely a word of peace for the suppliant, it has an aspiration of hope for the injurer. When enemies are in deplorable need of help, it is only the most mean and the most ungenerous who would refuse it. The man, for example, who, with power to aid his foe, would leave him to bleed on the field, — or who would deny him bread in his hunger, or drink in his thirst,— who would insult his gray hairs, or rejoice over the last grave of his posterity, — such a man would be execrated and despised by universal sympathy. And, should he do entirely the opposite to all this, his deeds would be considered as no transcendent virtue; it would be only what all men of ordinary humanity would do in such circumstances.

Though a man, therefore, should raise his enemy from the place of his fall, and heal up his wounds, — though he should feed and refresh him in his want, — though he should refuse to heap odium on his age, — though he should pity him in his solitude and bereavement, — he would not yet outstretch, to any extent, the limits of common charities. No, my friends, the trial is, to feel benevolently towards a prosperous enemy; to lament his malice, even while we suffer from it; to lament that his soul, in causing us unjustly to suffer, should do itself such a deadly and such a grievous wrong. It was in the temper of such mercy that Jesus wept over Jerusalem; it was in this temper that he sent the prayer to heaven from the tortures of the cross, "Father, forgive them." It was in this temper that Stephen's departing soul carried up the intercession, "Lay not this sin to their charge." It is never when the innocent is successful, but when he is defeated, that we behold the moral grandeur of his character. It is not when he has food, and drink, and clothing to bestow, but when he is himself in the thirst of death, or when he is cast wretched and homeless on the world, that we behold him in the fullness of his worth. It is then that the strength of duty is seen to rise above the strength of instinct; that the power of the soul is seen to rise above the power of the appetites; and that the spiritual man rules supremely over the earthly. Paul, in fetters before Felix, was grander than if clad in the purple of the Cæsars; and poor was the throne of their empire compared with the cross of Calvary.

3. The spirit of Christian forgiveness is magnanimous. We read in olden story of those who, when they gained a victory, dragged the unfortunate to their chariots. How much nobler are the conquerors who bear their honors meekly; but high above them all are

the heroic souls who refuse to pay back injury for injury. There are wrongs which are more cruel than death; yet is there a power in the gospel even superior to such wrongs. You rise to a heavenly sublimity of moral strength, when that power is yours,— yours in the face of accumulated provocation. Have you endured evils, — evils undeserved, — evils in return for good, — evils to the piercing of your heart and the destruction of your safety? Have you been the victim of injustice, which has haunted you with false accusation to the court of judgment? Has the calumniator followed you with stealthy pace, and wounded you in your dearest life? Have you been deserted — deserted in the hour of need — by those who should have been faithful to death? Has your friend betrayed you in the midst of enemies? All these our Saviour endured; he endured them to the cross; and on the cross the spirit of pardon was glorified.

The temper which retaliates an injury does not belong to a great mind or a good one. Suppose a case; let it contain all that it is the hardest to endure; the unkindness that cuts the soul; the injury that shocks the sense of right; let it be ingratitude which forgets generous assistance nobly given; let it be the violation of promises, the breach of trust, the betrayal of confidence; let it be a malice which, unable longer to conceal itself, follows its object with untiring hate,—a malice which has no hope but in the destruction of a benefactor, and which, for that purpose, concentrates all the forces of its cunning. See, then, this pursuer within grasp of the man for whose life he thirsted; and you behold David in the desert over the sleeping body of Saul! Passion would have given a fatal sentence; even prudence might have suggested an apology; opportunity favored its execution; one stroke of a poniard had avenged David's wrongs, and raised his ambition to a throne. Policy might have whispered that it was a dictate of wisdom; sophistry, that it was the judgment of heaven, — that it was the fulfilment of destiny. But, in the heart of David, feelings more honest were triumphant, and he was faithful to conscience and to truth. What sublimity do we cast around the fugitive, in an attitude of forbearance over the powerless body of his foe! but had a dangerous temptation prevailed over generous principle, how much the assassin would have sunk below the tyrant!

Vindictive action always turns the current of our sympathy; the injurer becomes the sufferer; the avenger then takes the place of the injurer, and loses all hold on our brotherly interest. He has sought compensation in his own way, and he must abide by what he has taken. Nay, when a man has once avenged an injury done him, he then becomes his own accuser ; he reviews his action with remorse, and he wishes it were not done ; but then his wishes are in vain, and the deed must continue fixed in the irrevocable past. When a man has fully avenged his own injury, he immediately becomes advocate for his adversary. His sympathies plead for *him*, while conscience accuses himself. He perceives the mitigations which soften the guilt of the transgressor, and he perceives as clearly the circumstances which aggravate his own. He falls in his own esteem; and he is conscious that he has lessened the esteem of others. He mourns that he had not more self-restraint ; that he had not more magnanimous resolution ; he is bowed under a sense of his unworthiness, and the memory of his unkindness. Satiety, in *other passions*, is the end of pleasure ; satiety in revenge is but the beginning of sorrows. It is not that others set us in place of the injurer ; we do it ourselves ; and the pain which we caused to him returns upon us a hundred-fold. It is thus that every evil passion becomes in itself a torment. It is odious to our inspection ; it is bitter in our experience ; promise what it will, its consummation is but wrath.

One may pretend to quiet in the sight of men ; he may justify himself with ingenious arguments, and with many words; but the irritation of his soul consumes him; with no consolation from Calvary, he endures the agony of crucifixion. In the sight of God and man, in the secret conviction of the soul, the forgiver has the award of righteousness, and he has the position of greatness. Is not the implacable spirit generally connected with some other unholy passion? Is it not the associate of disappointed avarice or ambition — often mere envy in a mask? It is, in many instances, not a man's fault, but his success, which creates the offence; not his demerit, but his superiority; because he has the power to excel, it is his misfortune to provoke those to whom none can be amiable, but such as have nothing to dispute, and to whose friendship, the best recommendation is subserviency or incapacity.

4. Let us consider what a blessed spirit is that of Christian forgiveness, of Christian mercy. It keeps us in the love of God, because it keeps us in his likeness God is our benign father, and He who is good to us all, commands us to be good to each other. In the degree we fulfill this command, we have confidence towards God; we can approach Him with simple trust, and we can ask with sincerity for that pardon which we have given. Never is the human heart more in the image of God, than when it pardons with a free and generous bounty; never does a man seem to tower up to the dignity and happiness of the Creator, more than

when he dispenses mercy, and foregoes every remembrance of his wrongs. This spirit living once within us, we know the deep love of Christ, and we enjoy communion with his exalted soul. We are enlarged with his divine expansion; we escape from the straitened selfishness, which seeks retaliation for every offence, and in retaliation finds but torture. We enjoy repose of soul; the passions that convulse it are not aroused, nay, they are conquered, and the affections govern in a tranquil reign. Our days are days of peace; the calm sky is a mirror of our experience; the sun gleaming in the quiet lake, is as the light of heaven in our thoughts. Our work proceeds in security, and it proceeds with effect; for our energies are not divided, and they are not disturbed. The face of man is pleasant to us, we are conscious of no malice, of no evil intention; and every man is, therefore, our brother.

If there be any who think hardly of us, we do not add to the evil by returning it; if there be any that wish us harm, we will not realize their wish by its reciprocation; if there be any who would do us wrong, we will not *anticipate* their action against ourselves, by doing to *them* the misdeed which they contemplate against *us*. We preserve the goodness of our hearts, and then we have the peace which cannot be taken from us. Like charity "mercy" never faileth. If we do good to them who hate us, we are doubly happy, and they have no power to hurt us. Mercy is from above: —

> "It droppeth as the gentle rain from heaven
> Upon the place beneath; it is twice blessed;
> It blesseth him that gives, and him that takes."

But how accursed is the spirit of hatred! the deadliest spirit and the worst, which the poet places in his Pandemonium of evil. Gloomily, she came upon the world, as smoke from the bottomless pit, shrouding the sun of heaven, and withering the beauty of earth. Onward she has trod her fearful way, the dark minister of terror. Her throat is an open sepulchre; with her tongue she uses deceit; the poison of asps is under her lips; her mouth is full of cursing and bitterness; her feet are swift to shed blood; destruction and misery are in her ways; the way of peace she has not known; there is no fear of God before her eyes. Hers it is to sow discord among brethren; hers to scatter party spirit and bigotry over the land; hers to make children of the same soil Cains to one another; hers to dash nation against nation, and to bury millions in the shock; hers to rejoice in evil as her *good*, and to glory when evil is *triumphant*. When domestic peace has fled the hearth; when tranquillity is banished from the neighborhood; when the avenger plunges the death-weapon in his opponent's bosom; when the incendiary purples the midnight with a sanguinary blaze; when the plain is reeking, and the city heaves in agony, and thrones tremble in the crash, — Hatred is there; there in ruthless fury; there in exulting malevolence; there amidst tribulation and anguish, feasting her soul on banquets of pain, and celebrating her conquest amidst misery and despair! O! may the power of Jesus expel her from the world! consume the fiend with the spirit of his mouth, and destroy her with the brightness of his coming!

II. What does the spirit of Christian forgiveness require of us, and by what motives may it be strengthened? This I can but briefly touch, and close.

1. It requires of us, forbearance; and not forbearance, simply, of outward action, but of inward feeling. There is this difference between the forgiving man, and the revengeful man, that the one finds pleasure in forgetting, and the other in remembering his wrongs; the one uses every exertion to diminish the sense of injury, and the other uses every exertion to increase it. It is a painful, and in truth, a self-crucifying disposition, which is compelled to linger on the dark side of things, and especially on such views of character as tend to foster gloomy sentiments. By leaving out of frequent

contemplation irritating recollections, we may do much to suppress such a tendency. One dark thought cherished in the mind, has an evil fecundity of others darker than itself. But the mind that turns from the evil to seek the good, will ever find sufficient to recompense its labor, and to mitigate its severity. And, granting that one's idea of an enemy's character should not be as evil as that character deserves, yet how much better is it, to preserve the simplicity of charity, than to nourish the prejudice of aversion; how much better to discern in the vague obscurity, floating images of good, than to magnify, by the mist of anger, every fault into gigantic stature.

The spirit of Christian forgiveness requires compassion as well as forbearance — not general compassion for the external misfortune of an enemy, simply, but compassion for his very enmity. And is there not a cause? If we conceive the unutterable delight of a genial and benignant temper, we must regard a vindictive disposition as a sad affliction, and we must pity the man who feeds the serpent which stings himself. We feel compassion in proportion to the height from which any being falls. No one, then, more needs it, than he who is the prey of uncharitable dispositions, for he descends the most from his heavenly origin, and becomes the most unlike a child of God. But the spirit of Christian forgiveness, can rise to positive good towards an enemy. A man, under its influence, would do justice to his enemy's merits; he would admit his virtues; make allowance for his weakness; defend his character; sympathize with his affliction; desire his happiness, and, if possible, aid him to attain it. He would thus try to make impression by the silent eloquence of elevated principle; he would prove, by his entire conduct, how superior charity is to pride; he would embrace every opportunity to remove misapprehension; he would fall upon the heart of his opponent with gentle droppings of kindness; and he would wear into his affections, though they were coated by a rock.

2. By what motives shall we actuate this spirit? The motives are as many as they are impressive. Our great fallibility ought, in the first place, to restrain our judgments. We are liable to mistakes, respecting others, even in their external life; we can but dimly see it; we behold it in remote perspective, and we hear of it with uncertain sound. How seldom do we discern an event in its several relations; how seldom have we any saying exactly as it was. If the outward life is thus partial to our apprehensions, how much beyond our vision is the inward. When we attempt to judge of this, how we must be mocked and baffled.

How can we read the heart! How can we see what may be there, which may falsify all our conjectures, and be the very contradictory of what we had supposed. How can we know in what a different light our words or deeds appeared to that heart, from what they seemed to ourselves! But, if we must be thus uncertain in our decision, how can we adjust the punishment? We may punish the innocent, or we may punish above measure.

Moreover, in both the judgment and the sentence, the court of inquiry, and the tribunal of allotment, are with ourselves: self-love presides, and passion argues. Alas, if conscience be not allowed the prerogative of revision, the case has but small chance of fairness. Nor is it incapacity, alone, that should restrain our severity, but also, the knowledge that our own sins have taken from us the title to deal vengeance. We are not qualified to be avengers, while we are in the deepest want of forbearance. The attitude of suppliants is more appropriate to us than that of inexorable accusers. Let any one, in a meditative hour, ask himself how constantly he needs to be regarded with a forbearing and benignant spirit; let him think how wretched he would be, if he did not meet this in his fellow-creatures; and he will arise, I apprehend, disposed to return the mercy he requires.

3. Let us think, too, of our common origin, and our common end. Children of one Father, shall any embitter the way to the home which he has prepared for them in heaven? Shall they pervert the powers of undying souls, to destroy each other's peace, and to work each other ill? Shall they, who are to live together in the existence of eternity, hate each other in the sojourn of a moment? In any great calamity, this common nature assumes its supremacy, and then divisions and disputes are lost in its immensity. Let shipwreck cast a number upon the perils of the waves, or the famine of the rocks; let an appalling danger unite them all in sorrow; and the most violent enemies are made brothers. Mortality and tears efface their disagreements. Behold the visitation of general disease! The feuds which disturbed a city are hushed; the spites and vanities that separated neighbors are heard no more; the insults which seemed unpardonable, are turned into puerile trifles; the adversaries that shunned each other in silent pride, address each other with sympathy and concern; a universal pardon takes place, in the humility of universal suffering. And yet, my brethren, the common lot of pain and death, though less violently, is quite as certainly proclaimed through every hour, and on every tomb. We are all as united in this awful destiny, as if Death met us in the roar of

the waters, or in the mortality of the plague; as surely are we all passing to one bourne, in our straggling isolations, as if we went together in bands of ten thousand each. Silently, affliction is in the shadows of life; without noise is death pacing the chambers of the merry world; without any visible consternation, humanity is swept from the surface of the earth. Why should we then wrangle? Why rather should we not aid each other? Why should not our solemn duties, and our hastening end, render us so united, that personal contention would be impossible, in a general sympathy, quickened by the breath of a forbearing and pitying charity.

DAVID: SPIRITUAL INCONGRUITIES.

1 Sam. xvii. 58.

SAUL SAID UNTO HIM, WHOSE SON ART THOU, YOUNG MAN? AND DAVID ANSWERED, I AM THE SON OF THY SERVANT JESSE, THE BETHLAMITE.

"History," it has been remarked, "is philosophy teaching by example;" but history teaches truly, only so far as we conceive justly of the events and characters which it describes. And, indeed, as modern writers generally describe the remote Past, it is extremely difficult to gather from their smooth narrations any just ideas of things or persons as they really were. Most modern writers *translate* — so to speak — distant ages into the dialect of their own, and they ascribe motives and designs to ancient characters, which have no more fitness than if *we* were to paint their persons in *our* costume. We ought to be transported to the time which we would study, by the force of a moral and sympathetic imagination. We ought to cast our existence into the midst of its passions and its interests; and our existence, for the while, should take the shape of these passions, and the fashion of these interests. It is a noble exercise of our noblest faculties, to call into renovated being the transcendent men whom the memory of humanity has canonized. It is as exalting as it is instructive, to clothe them again by fancy, in flesh and blood, to hear their serious voices, and to listen to their august and solemn wisdom. It is an enlargement of our own existence, to question the centuries which have gone, and to *compel* them to reveal to us the knowledge which enriched them. It is an influence fraught with the deepest inspiration, to enter into the life of departed ages; to converse with those who originated or governed their grand activities, — to converse with them, not as dim and distant shadows, but as real and bodily men, — to converse with them as formed by the circumstances of their nation and their day.

I have tried myself, in this way of study, to apprehend the character of David. I have tried to enter into his age, and into his surrounding circumstances; to look upon him as a great, inspired, tempted, sorrowing soul; and in this spirit I shall try to speak of him. I shall try to speak of him with sympathy, with truth, with admiration, with reverence, yet with sadness also. Let no hearer, therefore, misunderstand me. David was a *prophet*, but I shall speak most of him as a *man*;

and I desire most to call your attention to him in his actual and his merely human life. This it will be my effort to briefly sketch, and, as I sketch it, to connect such reflections with the statement as arise naturally out of the incidents.

Saul had fallen under the denunciation of Samuel. His fate was sealed beyond the power of repentance. He was prophetically rejected from being king over Israel. A hero in spirit and in life, warlike and ambitious, loss of power was the heaviest affliction he feared or could endure. At once passionate and superstitious, he sank under the words of the stern priest. He lost his tranquillity and he lost his trust. Alternately he became the prey of fury and of despondency.

It was in an hour when the fitful storm brooded most darkly over his mind, that a youth was introduced to his presence, — a shepherd youth, that drew from the harp of Israel its holiest and its sweetest sounds, a most gracious music, that fell as a voice from heaven upon the morbid feelings of the monarch, and charmed that agitated breast into repose, — that morbid breast to which peace had been long a stranger. That youth was David, — David, the rustic boy; David, yet free, and ardent, and happy; David, yet pure in his enthusiasm, yet throbbing with incipient poetry, with innocent affections, with patriotic ardor, with every generous desire. This great and gifted youth comes from his pastoral retreats. And he also is to be a king. He also is to feel convulsions deeper than those which he came to soothe. He also is to sit and mourn in a midnight which has no star to cheer it. He also is to seek for solace, when his heart is sad, yet find none at hand to give it. He, the joyous and elastic lad, is to bow down his head in anguish, to water his couch with tears, to mingle his bread with ashes, to clothe his soul in sackcloth, to be as a sparrow on the house-top, to be as a pelican in the wilderness, to glitter in the midst of royalty and state; but to bear in secret every torture of a wounded spirit, yet find none who could minister to a mind diseased, — to feel companionless in the multitude, and despairing when alone, — to tremble in darkness, and to fear the light.

The opening of David's public course glows with sublime ardor, and is full of heroism. Goliah, the champion of the Philistines, mighty in stature and swelled up in pride, challenged the hosts of Israel for a man that could oppose him. Well might they stand in consternation. They were before an exulting and powerful enemy. They were enfeebled, they were humiliated; having lost obedience, they had lost their courage. Unbelieving towards their God, they had become cravens towards their country.

The stripling, David, comes forth in this dismay. He is asked to clothe himself in heavy armor, but he will not have it. His friends would try to invest him with strong weapons, but he will none of them. He has no hope in brute force. He has no hope in animal contention. He knows that, within these terms, all odds are against him; and he looks for power to higher and better sources. A few stones and a sling, these are all that he will take. He will go forward against presumptuous self-confidence. He understood *where* the noblest strength lay, and nobly he used it. He showed what the whole history of man exhibits, — that faith in divine protection, that devotion to conscience, that intellectual skill, that moral enthusiasm, can trample down resistance, however gigantic.

What is muscle at any time against mind? What is passion against belief? What is frenzied anger against deliberative conviction? Reverence and Reason are the true conquerors of the earth. To them belong the victory, and to them belong dominion. David stands out, as a *type* of this great power. The monster fell dead before his missile, and he, the victor, has left a record for our learning, to reveal to us, for everlasting ages, what is the potency of the gifted and the inspired mind. David's victory over Goliah is but a prophetic condensation of what true minds have been doing ever since; and all that the noblest minds have done, to subdue the antagonisms of passion and of matter, are foreshadowed in this action of David's. He may be placed as the deathless incarnation of what trust and thought can accomplish against tyranny and force.

Success, however, must pay its penalty. Distinction must meet the spectral shadow of envy on its path. It must find the sunshine dimmed by grim distortion. David fared as greatness has fared in every period. He encountered malice where he earned gratitude. By the amount of obligations which he conferred, he provoked the dislike which never pardons; and by the applause which he inspired, he became odious to the vanity that can tolerate all things in others except their merit. He had only the destiny of his class. The acclamations of his countrymen drew upon him the hatred of his sovereign. He endured that hatred with untiring fortitude. He made it the return of a magnanimous forbearance. Twice he stood over his sleeping enemy, and twice he refused to purchase by a stroke security and a crown.

This was the brightest era of David's life. Stained it was with the evils of his time, but yet it was ennobled by heroic virtues and by manly affections. And of these his purest was the friendship for

Jonathan. But Jonathan was worthy, most worthy of the strongest and the most lasting affection. There was in the character of Jonathan an inexpressible attraction, a most winning sweetness, a rare union of mildness and strength, of courage and repose. Dutiful to his father, he was faithful to his friend. Admitting his parent's rights, he did not partake his passions. He gave to Saul, through all his fury, the obedience of a subject and the reverence of a son. Still he is faithful to David; true to him in danger, loyal to him in distress, protecting him with sleepless vigilance, adhering to him with unabated love. Withal, he does not desert his father. He was near him ever. He hovered around him, like a guardian spirit. He lingered under the shadow of his fate. And when at last the hour of destiny came, he was struggling by his father's side, and there in valiant combat he gave forth his breath. Short in his career, cut off in the midst of his days, gentle in his life, brave in his death, well did he deserve the lamentation which David uttered, — "O, Jonathan, slain on thine own mountains; I am in distress for thee, my brother Jonathan, very dear wast thou to me; wonderful was thy love unto me, passing the love of women; how have the mighty fallen!"

David was one of those great and original men,

whom humanity at rare intervals produces. His mind was of that order which creates the age in which it lives, and that saves or destroys the nation which it rules. His character was that which Time, if it would, is not able to kill; that which History is forced to remember. It is the destiny of transcendent power, whether it be good or whether it be bad, to leave everlasting impression on the affairs of mankind. David was a man of power, various and exalted. Strong in intellect, and wise in experience; strong in will, and commanding in expression; strong in every attribute which *compels* obedience, he was accomplished also in the qualities that win it. Poetry, music, architecture, he loved with extreme desire; he advanced them with a noble zeal. Poetry, in sweetest melody and in boldest flight, — music, in the inspired simplicity of its early youth, — he loved and practised with the most passionate enthusiasm. Architecture, too, was familiar to him in the utmost splendor of original conception; for it was he who designed the temple of Jerusalem, though it was his son Solomon who carried the design into execution.

When we consider the obscurity from which David was drawn, the majesty of his ideas and his deeds must strike us with exceeding admiration. In the heroes of antiquity there is no man that can approach comparison with him ; and still less has he any parallel in the most magnificent impersonations of our modern life. In some points he resembled Bonaparte. Like Bonaparte, he arose from the people, and sat upon his throne by their will ; like Bonaparte, his people adored him, and would endure to the last extremity of human nature for his interest. Like Bonaparte, he was a conqueror. His circumstances were created by the age, and not by himself. He had to meet and to subdue them as best he could. He was forced into fight, and fight he did, with most electric courage and decision. With his most rapid genius, he flashed defeat upon his enemies before they were aware of his approach. The necessity to fight indulged the disposition to fight ; one victory led to another ; and as he acquired territory by the sword, he increased it and he enlarged it more and yet more.

Like Bonaparte, he was a dictator. He had, to be sure, his great and mighty men, for he knew, by the glance of a look, the man who was born to control his associates ; and as he knew the man, he selected him. The great and mighty men of both were subordinates, but not competitors ; and herein consisted the greatness of both, that they had power to make them subordinates. Like Bonaparte, he was a legislator. He gave his people laws, and he established among them a settled and systematic administration. But he had a piety, and a faith, and devotional sensibility, of which the mighty modern had not a single impulse.

There is another modern, to whom David also bears, in some degree, a resemblance, — Peter the Great, of Russia. David, as Peter, found only barbarism in the land; but ere he died, it was exalted and civilized. The great king of Israel, as the great czar of Russia, was the patron of every art, and the friend of every genius who could raise his country into prosperity and dignity. He found his brethren dwelling in tents; he departed from among them living in palaces. He found them scattered tribes; he left them a collected and compacted nation. He found them diggers and herdsmen; he left them heroes and princes. The desert disappeared, and where the thorn and the thistle grew, there sprung the vine, and the olive tree, and the wheat field: and from them, wine, that makes man glad, and oil, that gives him a cheerful countenance, and bread, that strengthens his heart. Where the sight met nothing but solitary waste, he caused the adorned city to spring up; and he strengthened it for war, and he beautified it for peace. Under the guidance of his stupendous mind, the land was filled with plenty, the sea was covered with commerce, literature was encouraged, industry was successful, victory waited on arms, and wisdom prevailed in counsel.

If we contrast David with Saul, David appears as superior as heaven is to earth. It is superiority, not of an improved succession, but of a new creation. Saul, like David, was exalted from common to kingly life. Saul, like David, was a man of battle, and a man of blood; — and here the resemblance closes. To the end, Saul was only the savage warrior, a man of might and daring, a man of prowess and enthusiasm. This agrees fully with his personal qualities, and is in nowise opposed to his original condition. It is all that we might imagine, and our expectations are neither surpassed nor contradicted. Commanding in the qualities which make a man of war, David had, in more signal perfection, those which in a better period would have made a man of peace. Distinguished by his valor, he was yet more ennobled by attributes, without which valor is but brutal impulse: by patriotism, by piety, by the zeal with which he maintained the institutions of religion, and by the prophet-poetry with which he inspired the services of the tabernacle. Powerful in mind, in will, in action, in passion, his character is most decided, and his crimes are as marked as his virtues.

If we pass from the incidents of David's life to the spirit of it, we have subject for frequent and profound reflection.

The history of David leaves one impression on the mind deeply and plainly ; and that is, that moral principle does not always correspond with devotional sensibility. I do not say that devotional sensibility is not a fine element in moral action ; nay, I hold, that without it, the highest beauty is wanting to character and to virtue. But still, devotional sensibility may be found in many persons, who are weak in right principles, and unstable in right purposes. How fervently could David pray, but how feebly did David practice! What more excellent than his sentiments, what more condemnable than his passions! How sublimely could his spirit mount to heaven, but how terribly could he wrong his neighbor! Strange, indeed, are the inconsistencies of our nature. One part of a man's life will seem, often, the direct reverse of another. Who would have thought that David could ever have incurred the guilt he did? Who could have thought that David, who, in the first days of his life, gave his heart to poetry, and filled his solitude with music, would afterwards so defile his hands with blood, and so cover his spirit with impurity?

Yet David was not really insincere. It is well and wisely written, — The heart is deceitful above all things; who can know it? Much and strange contradiction there is in life, but less of positive hypocrisy than is imagined. David is a type of many kings and many men. The example, in this character which Scripture gives us, is ever and ever repeated in history; and it is as often corroborated in daily life. We read in history — do we not? — of monarchs, who could tremble in the pangs of conscience, as the preacher denounced the judgments of God against the unrighteous, yet whose tears might be said, almost without a figure, to have been dried in the harlot's smile. We read of monarchs who could carry on most guilty wars, — who, in blind, relentless, and inhuman obstinacy, could prolong the contest, — who, deaf to weeping and careless of suffering, destroyed as many at home by oppression as abroad by the sword; yet some of these monarchs were religious. They were religious; not indeed with an elevated religion, but yet not with any assumed or pretended zeal. They were not hypocrites; nay, in their way, they were earnestly sincere. And in our own experience, how changeful and uncertain are our characters? In an hour we passionately resolve, and in another as recklessly break our resolution. To-day, pray with weeping and contrition, and to-morrow forget that God yet lives who heard us then; yes, by both consciousness and observation, we know that guilt and folly may disorder a life, which has also in it fountains of religious sensibility. Instability and inconsistency there are in this, but sincerity there is in it also.

The real philosophy of the matter is, that the religious element, like the other elements of our nature, must be good or bad, as it is directed. By the religious element I mean, in this connection, the faculty which connects us with the invisible and eternal world; and this, directed by ignorance and passion, may do, without remorse, deeds that have no name, but, influenced by knowledge and by benignity, raises a man, not simply to be a little lower than the angels, but to be their equal and their companion. But the merely devotional man is not necessarily a virtuous man; nay, he is not necessarily a benevolent man; he may fail in rectitude, or he may fail in humanity. Of this principle, the whole history of the church gives sufficient evidence: for many a devout man has been dishonest, and many a devout man has been cruel. I do not join in the common cry which stigmatizes all such as hypocrites. I do not believe that the failings of those, on whom the world charged inconsistency, always sprung from deceit; I simply believe that they were men of partial development, and that, in the exaggerated expression of some faculties, others were disproportionately, and thence injuriously, weakened. The mere devotional sentiment will not, in itself, protect a man against the temptations of the malignant passions, as is sufficiently witnessed in many a decent calumniator, and in every conscientious persecutor. Neither will the devotional sentiment, in itself, guard a man against the temptations of the lower desires. It did not in the case of David, and this we have to lament the more on account of the real grandeur of his soul.

Wickedness there is abundantly in the world, and so far there is, in the world, a universal subject and cause of grief. But, when sin unites with noble gifts, it is exceeding sinful. When it puts convulsion into the heart in which there burned the sacred fire of God; when it throws a foul blot upon the light sent as a gift from above to guide millions in the ways of righteousness; when it disorders the heavenward spirit; when it casts down the sons of the morning from their Empyrean height, and leaves them to grope their degraded way in nether darkness; when it makes the life uncertain, which would have been our trust; when it makes the conduct false, which would have been our comfort; when it prostrates the generous and the loving, on whom we could have spent our most prodigal affections; we behold sin, then, as the darkest enemy, and we start from it in fear, while we weep for it in sorrow. Very sinful, indeed, were periods in the life of David. But many were the tears which he shed upon his guilt, and in these tears of agony and remorse they are written for our learning.

Let me offer a few words, — a few words on that blood-guiltiness, for which some men, through David, assault the Bible.

We are to judge David as we judge other men, by his times and by his circumstances. His age was one of rudeness and it was one of blood. It was a period when men got readily into conflict, and when conflict was associated with little that was forbearing or magnanimous. The barbarian instincts to contention were those which then were the most developed. The passions which create war were ever active and constantly provoked, and the sentiments which mitigate it were but slightly felt. Prowess was the great test of excellence. Might was the principle of right. The military hero was "the highest style of man." The conqueror, the subduer, was the king of men, and none besides could rule them. By the sword dominion was obtained, and by the sword dominion was defended. David was certainly a man of battle, but what else could he be, and be a king in the period in which he lived? Shall we make that David's sin, which was David's fate? Did David choose to be a king? Was he not a warrior by the necessity of events, rather than by any personal contrivance? Did he feel no sorrow for the evils to which his destiny carried him? Did he make no moans? Did he weep no tears? Surely he did. Often was his heart cast down, and often his rest was broken. Much he lamented that he was a man of blood, and with that soiled and terrible red hand of his, he would not venture to found a house for the worship of his Maker.

What else could his life have been, but that of warfare? By what means could he have avoided being, throughout his course, a warrior? He was on all sides surrounded by enemies, by enemies to his nation and to his religion; by enemies, ever-watchful, and ever-cruel — therefore, he had ever to fight for defence, and victory was needful to security. He entered on a distracted kingdom, and he became heir to unfinished battles. Saul had ever been in contention, and he left his successor a legacy of complicated hostilities. But, with the many and sad sins of David, there still remained in his nature, much that was great and lofty, a tenderness that strife could not wholly destroy, a piety, sublime, however defaced and darkened, a sense of duty, a spirit of repentance, a yearning for the right, a wisdom prepared for all emergencies, a dignity which no turn of affairs could degrade, and which preserved him, manly and self-sustained, in every affliction and every misfortune.

David's career was splendid and successful. From a few pastoral and agricultural tribes, as I have already noticed, he raised a glorious nation. Its homes had multiplied, its stalls were filled with cattle, its hills were covered with plenty, its borders were enlarged, and beyond them it was respected as well as feared. David's station was the highest that earth affords. He had gifts the holiest that God bestows. Was he happy? Was he greatly happy? Was he even moderately happy? When David sat upon the throne of Israel, when he lodged in his house of cedar, when his enemies were subdued, when his fame was spread from Egypt to Lebanon, and from Lebanon to the sea, did he never think regretfully on the youthful son of Jesse? Did he never recall, in melancholy vision, the green pastures and the still waters, where his breast was calm, and where his step was free; where his hopes were peaceful, and where his thoughts were gay; where the lonely valley listened to his song, and where the evening breeze carried forth the music of his maiden harp?

David was not a happy man. Despondency settled on his soul, and calamities, treading fast upon each other, haunted all his latter days. Often, indeed, did he mingle his drink with weeping; often did he take ashes for bread; often to him the day was dark, and the night was heavy; often at the dawn did he wish for the evening, and at the evening sigh again for the dawn. He is an example that no grandeur, no prosperity, no impunity from station, no glory of command, no flattery of obedience, can strips sin of its hatefulness, or rob it of its sting. He is an example, that there is a law more sacred than the voice of kings, a law which that voice, terrible as it sometimes is, cannot subvert; that there is a power more awful than human royalty, which royalty itself cannot escape; that such power from the humblest lips, can strike, at times, the proudest souls with terror; that within a thousand walls of iron, that within a thousand shields of adamant, that within a thousand ranks of arms, guilty kings have, with all their state, no shelter; that God's eye is on the monarch as the beggar; that in the depth of millions their transgression can find them out; and that, in the stern truth of God's own sentence, it can shriek within their conscience the terrible rebuke of divine condemnation. Nathan said to David, "Thou art the man." Within David's own heart there was a speech that told him, what man he was. The earthquake or the tempest could not have drowned the distinctness of that stunning voice; the jewelled garment of the prince, the mailed armor of the soldier, was no defence against the barbed arrow of conviction that pierced and quivered within the stricken breast.

David, too, is an evidence, if evidence were wanted, that grandeur is a poor shelter against grief. When shame fell upon David's house, when hatred placed one child in deadly feud against another, the glare of royalty was a small matter in the sadness of nature. When, retreating from the unnatural rebellion of his son, the curses of Shimei fell heavy on his bended head, what was there in the name of king to meeken the storm which beat upon his anointed person? The fatal mistake is ever to put the office above the nature; for the nature is changeless and must triumph. The office is for man, and not man for the office; circumstances make the office, but God has made the man. The man is, therefore, greater than king or than priest. What was kingship to the English Charles, when, after arraignment before his own people, he clasped his children for the last time to his bosom, before his going to the block? What was kingship to the French Louis, when he felt he must leave his helpless wife and orphans to the mercies of the mad avengers who began in his own blood the retaliation for centuries of suffering, which was only to be accomplished in a wilderness of death? What was kingship to David, when his own flesh were his enemies? There is rebellion in the land. His throne totters; the throne, so hardly won, rocks upon its foundation; there is a palsy of desolate affliction, that never, never, never, again, shall let a smile glimmer on his face. His hoary hairs are dragged rudely towards the grave, the staff of his earthly hope, and pride, and joy is broken; and he, crowned as he is, falls upon the bare bosom of adversity, to endure its chill, until he can endure no longer.

And who causes all this? Absalom, the beloved, Absalom, the beautiful! O, foolish and most guilty youth, what a true and loving father didst thou dare with thy hand of sacrilege, and thy treachery of blood! Yet, hear how the heart of the father speaks out in David. "Deal gently," he says to the commanders, as they go out to battle, "deal gently, for my sake, with the young man, even with Absalom." Behold him, then, when his crown, his state, his very life, is in danger. How eagerly he inquires of those who bring tidings from the field; how he catches at every gleam of hope; how he watches each moment for reports; and when the messenger at last arrives, for what does he inquire? His sceptre — his throne? No. Is the young man Absalom safe? This is his first, this is his special question.

The young man Absalom had gone to his last account! What was the world, then, to David, and what was all that the world contained? What, then, were thrones or dominions, or principalities or powers? The spirit of the man, the spirit of the father, was greater than all. Officials murmured and rebuked; but what were their murmurs and rebukes to his torn and broken heart? Unheeding these ungenial words, "he went up to the chamber over the gate, and wept; and as he went, he said, — O, my son, Absalom, my son, my son! would God, I had died for thee, my son, my son!"

I have spoken of David as I proposed, as one within the circle of our imperfect humanity, and I have spoken of him in the spirit of humanity. In this spirit I view in him an incarnation of its capacities, and an example of its weakness. In this spirit, I cannot think of him otherwise than in solemn reverence and solemn sorrow. With this solemn sorrow and solemn reverence, I contemplate his mighty mind; with reverence I see its grandeur; with sorrow I behold its fall from that grandeur, to wilder itself in madness, or to lose itself in folly. So likewise I contemplate his courageous and capacious heart, so bold and yet so gentle, so made for truth and love, so fraught with sublime emotion and humble piety, transformed to a chaos of passion, convulsed to a volcano of impure and unholy desires. With awe I gaze on his superhuman imagination; with rapture I hear his heaven-born utterance. With equal awe I behold him in his fearful trials, his said temptations, his unwonted sorrows, in the miseries of his sin, in the miseries of his remorse. I learn how strength may work for wretchedness, how privileges may turn to penalties. Looking upon David comprehensively, in his greatness, in his abasement, in repentance, in his guilt, in his aspiration, in his affliction, I am reminded of his own words, suggested doubtless by his own experience — "Verily, every man at his best estate is altogether vanity!"

David has been by many considered a type of Christ. This is a bold use of allegorical interpretation: for if there are some external analogies, there is a complete spiritual contrast. Christ was of David's tribe — but surely was not of David's mind. David was a king — Christ also was a king. But Christ was not a king by the sword, by conquest, or in outward state. Christ was not a king by coercing men, but by attracting them; he was not a king by resistance, but by endurance. His sway was over the soul, and by love and not by fear; it was inward — it was of heaven; it ruled the highest thoughts, and it promised nothing, and it gave nothing to the lower passions. David was a prophet; but too frequently the lips touched with the fire of the sanctuary, were moved with the fury of the camp; too frequently David's sojourn was in Mesech, and his dwelling in the tents of Kedar. Christ was a prophet, more divinely called. He was a prophet of perfect peace; grace and mercy the mission of his life, they were the testament of his death. He walked over earth in meekness; being reviled, he reviled not again, but committed himself to God, who judgeth righteously. Not breaking the bruised reed, nor quenching the smoking flax, surrounded by malice and by madness, he passed through suffering on to victory.

David was a monarch, and a hero; and some who called Christ the son of David, would have made him, too, a monarch and a hero. Little did they know of Christ's kingdom, little could they understand of his heroism. Nothing wist they of that reign, which commenced when it seemed to close; a reign destined to be of wider space than that which the sun enlightens, and to live with the everlasting soul when many suns shall quench with age. Little did they think, that, in dark Gethsemane, in the torture of bloody sweat, a glory was born which could never die; that a traitor-kiss saluted the sublimest of sovereigns; that a rabble shout, meant in mockery, proclaimed the most lasting of dominions; that a wreath of thorns was a crown more unfading than a diadem, in which every nation had planted a jewel; that a cross, whereon a harassed soul lingered slowly to immortality, was a throne of loftier majesty than that which David founded, and than that which Solomon ascended.

David was a man of action, and a man of thought. Great he was as either, but far greater he was as the latter than the former. As a man of action, he belonged to his own age; as a man of thought, he is for all ages. As a man of action, he was for the Jewish people; as a man of thought, he is for the entire church, for the church enduring and universal. Of that church he has continued to be the deathless lyrist. David, of the throne, we cannot always recall with pleasure. David, of the psalms, we never would forget. David, of the psalms, the heart of Christendom cherishes, and will cherish always. The psalms are an everlasting manual to the soul; the book of its immortal wishes, its troubles, its aspirations, and its hopes: sung in every tongue, and in every age; destined to endure, while the universe of God has light, harmony, or grandour, while man has religion or sensibility, while language has sublimity or sweetness.

Amongst all compositions, these alone deserve the name of sacred lyrics. These alone contain a poetry that meets the spiritual nature in all its moods and in all its wants, which strengthens virtue with glorious exhortations, gives angelic eloquence to prayer, and almost rises to the seraph's joy in praise. In distress and fear, they breathe the low, sad murmur of complaint; in penitence, they groan with the agony of the troubled soul. They have a gentle music for the peace of faith; in adoration, they ascend to the glory of creation, and the majesty of God. For assemblies or for solitude, for all that gladdens and all that grieves, for our heaviness and despair, for our remorse and our redemption, we find in these divine harmonies the loud or the low expression. Great has been their power in the world. They resounded amidst the courts of the tabernacle; they floated through the lofty and solemn spaces of the temple. They were sung with glory in the halls of Zion; they were sung with sorrow by the streams of Babel. And when Israel had passed away, the harp of David was still awakened in the church of Christ. In all the eras and ages of that church, from the hymn which first it whispered in an upper chamber, until its anthems filled the earth, the inspiration of the royal prophet has enraptured its devotions, and ennobled its rituals.

And thus it has been, not alone, in the august cathedral or the rustic chapel. Chorused by the winds of heaven, they have swelled through God's own temple of the sky and stars; they have rolled over the broad desert of Asia, in the matins and vespers of ten thousand hermits. They have rung through the deep valleys of the Alps, in the sobbing voices of the forlorn Waldenses; through the steeps and caves of Scottish highlands, in the rude chauntings of the Scottish covenanters; through the woods and wilds of primitive America, in the heroic hallelujahs of the early pilgrims.

Nor is it in the congregation, alone, that David has given to the religious heart a voice. He has given an utterance, also, for its privacy,— for the low-lying invalid, — soothing the dreariness of pain, softening the monotony of heavy time, supplying the prayer or the promise, with which to break the midnight or the sleepless hour: for the unhappy, to give them words of sadness, by which to relieve their disquieted and their cast-down souls; by which to murmur between themselves and God, the holy sorrow, that heaven alone should hear: for the penitent, when the arrows of conviction rankle in his breast, when the light of grace would seem departed, and the ear of mercy closed,— then David gives the cry of his own impassioned deprecation, in supplication and confession. And when contrition has found repose, and the tempest of lamentation been stilled by the assurance of peace, he gives the hymn of his exultant and of his grateful praise.

THE WEARINESS OF LIFE.

JONAH iv. 8.

IT IS BETTER FOR ME TO DIE THAN TO LIVE.

THIS was the desire of Jonah, when the Lord smote his gourd so that it died. In the disappointment of his soul he wept over it, and in the trouble of his spirit his prayer was for death. It is so with not a few selfish people. They can bear well the calamities that lay others low, even those that spread waste and death over nations; but let sorrow come near themselves, let it blight but a single joy in their home, touch any thing that is theirs, and they are overwhelmed. They seem to feel, to think, and to act, as if all the agencies of life and Providence are in motion but for them; and as if all were out of order when they suffer inconvenience, and all rightly going on when they are in comfort.

This estimate of ill-being, or well-being, in its relation to self, has always appeared to me extremely low; and yet it often takes a religious form of expression. Why should we thank God in phrases which imply that we have been measuring our own privileges with our fellow-creatures' disadvantages? That is not the tone in which to bless that God who is an impartial and an equal Father, who causes his sun to rise on the evil and the good, and sendeth his rain on the just and on the unjust. And why, also, should we regard calamities in any way peculiar or severe, because they come near to *us*? It is natural, indeed, that we should *feel* them more, but that is no reason why we should ever ascribe to them any other than their common character. But this distinction you will ever observe through life, — the selfish make little of the sufferings which their neighbors have to bear, however great, while they are loud about their own, however small. This other distinction you will equally observe, — the sufferings of the selfish render them more selfish; the sufferings of the generous make them more generous. The one class, under trials, become harder, and the other more impressible and affectionate. There are, however, many instances in which the weariness of Jonah may fall upon the spirit without his bitterness, and without his misanthropy. Many a one, with a sincerer despondency, is ready to exclaim with him, "It is better for me to die than to live."

How often is this the sentiment under severe physical pain, whether it is uttered or concealed? It is an awful test of resignation to have the whole frame shattered and disorganized; the head throbbing on the burning pillow, and a crushing load heavy on the heart; thoughts dancing giddily in the brain, and chaotic coloring disturbing the imagination; with no rest during the lingering and languid night, and no relief with the morning sun. How natural it is, in the tossings of convulsive irritation, to fix the mind upon the quiet grave! When some sailor has been whirled long upon the storm, rolling in gloom and hurricanes amidst ocean billows, working and watching until nature fails, how does he not yearn for some sheltered nook on shore, where, fearless of the tempest, he may lay him down to rest, and find whereon to place his weary head, and sleep? With as strong a desire, many a tired sufferer exclaims with Jonah, "It is better for me to die than to live."

It is very affecting when such experience enters the mind while existence is yet new. In truth, it is a sentiment that is rarely felt by the aged. Life seems to become more precious as it becomes later: as in the case of the Sybil's leaves, the less of it that remains, the more it grows in value. With some, this may be from habit, with others, it is from feeling; but whether from habit or feeling, it is good evidence that life has been, on the whole, desirable. The longer we stay in it, the greater the tenacity with which we cling to it. That it should be so, is in the order of causes. While we are young, we are more a part of the world than observers of it. The living life about us swallows up our life ; and the outward creation is incorporated with both our own life and the general life. The blood is quick and the brain busy, and with the actions of these all other motions and objects are confounded, and we do not so much *contemplate* as *live* them.

But, as the sense of being grows in calmness, we put society and nature distinctly out before us, and our interest in both we only begin to understand when we look at them from a point of rest. The feeling is a simple one, and we often have feelings like it. Returning, at the close of a fine autumn day, from a pedestrian excursion among the hills, some few will, at times, get on before the party ; they sit down on a rising ground, dwell silently on the declining light, turn their thoughts on the events and scenes which they passed through in excitement, watch the stragglers that follow, and exchange words of friendly reminiscence with the companions that are about them. Thus the aged stop as they cross the summit of life, and mark on the border of the dark valley the line of light, take more notice of the region in which they have been breathing, review the incidents, activities, and spaces through which they have travelled, and find that much there was which it was pleasant to have known, and that much there still remains which it is painful to leave. The world seems to be more hospitable as we prepare to quit it; it is like departing from our native land. Other climes may be brighter, more fertile, more lovely, more wise, more free, in every way more goodly, but our native land none of them can be. They cannot give us mother memories, they cannot give us back our youth, or the dreams of our youth. No; the land that opens for us a grave, can never be to us as the land that supported for us a a cradle.

Not unlike are the feelings with which this near creation acts on us, as life advances. We are used to these skies, and clouds, and lights. The sun is our pleasant acquaintance; the moon we have never ceased to love; we count the stars, and call them by their names. Seas, rivers, continents, climates, we come to be familiar with in our journeyings; but they were the studies also of our school-day hours. We have watched and waited for each season; had for each our tempers, our feelings, and our toils, and after each our memories and impressions. No; earth is not ungentle or ungracious; and every honest heart must feel a pang to depart from it. It is a home; we are used to it; it has the trees that we delight in; the flowers that we love; the people that we know; and the roof over it, the kindly and familiar heavens. Other spheres of the universe may be grander, more glorious, more blessed, more beautiful; but this is our native planet, its atmosphere the breath of our lives, its objects the images of our thoughts; dear to us by all that is sacred in remembrance or in affection. These are human emotions, and he who formed the human heart will not account them guilty.

But, if the love of life is stronger in age, the consciousness of life is stronger in youth. This very strength of consciousness may, and sometimes does, turn into a disgust of life. Having not deeply entered into the moral purposes of life, any thing which cuts off the young from its sparkling felicities, cleaves them almost to despair. When confinement or solitude becomes the lot of those whose joy is in action and a throng, in the freedom of God's works and seasons, there seems no more on earth for them to hope. When youth is crushed by misfortune or disease, it is then, of all times, that prolonged life would be regarded as most dreary. The tenderness of friends may have a genial influence; youthful piety may teach a quiet resignation; the first harassing trials once over, a solemn thoughtfulness, a holy elevation of soul may come, and often it does come, and beam upon the young brow like the rays of a celestial glory.

It is a fine thing to see a young man in the noon of his strength; it is a lovely sight to behold a young maiden in the glow of her beauty; but it is finer to see a young man bear lingering disease with a meek and uncomplaining heroism; and to behold a young maiden fading with saintly trust out of earth and into heaven, is a far lovelier sight than her beauty in its freshest bloom. But sometimes youth has no wise goodness at hand to instruct it; no vigilant tenderness around to solace, to cherish it; no loving consolation to speak to it in gracious words; no piety in itself to give it support and strength; and then poor nature has only weariness and discontent. Whither shall it turn, frail and exhausted heart? Crushed and clouded, in what shall it find rest? Where shall it seek for light? The dreams of earth have melted, the hopes of earth are gone; it has nothing before it, like the prophet, but the ashes of its gourd. The things that blossomed with luxuriance, the things that promised a rich fruition, had a worm in the core, and they begin to wither ere the sun has well risen. What is for the stricken heart? Nothing beneath the skies; it must look up beyond them from the dust, and find its treasures where the moth doth not corrupt.

A man may see his fortune moulder, and this is not without sore affliction. In our condition of society, say what we may, poverty is not only a misfortune, it is a heavy disadvantage. It requires a stout heart to bear it manfully; it requires a believing heart to bear it meekly. And many a one could bear it both manfully and meekly, if he had only to bear it alone. But this is rarely the case. Sorrows do not come alone to a man; and a man seldom comes alone to sorrow. To the utmost verge of the space a man occupies in life, his adversity will surround him with fellow-sufferers; and there will be those who press near to his heart, and whose silent looks are worse to him than tortures. That philosophy of Satan in the Book of Job is not true, when he says, "All that a man hath will he give for his life." On the contrary, a man would often give his life first of all, sooner than some that he holds precious should bear things that are hard and grievous to be borne. When a man beholds the fabric of his exertions levelled, in which he had treasured many expectations, in which he had garnered up his hopes; when he sees provisions for his family gone, and nothing but destitution awaiting those for whose sake he labored early, and late took rest, those who hung on him in infancy and looked to him in youth; when he foresees year after year coming with increased difficulties, — however the happy may wonder, however the wise may rebuke, however religion may forbid it, or virtue overcome it, — the prophet's wish will sometimes rise in his breast, and tremble on his lips — "It is better for me to die than to live."

But this is not the worst. The loss of this world's good may doubtless fall heavy on the spirit, but the wound, though deep, is seldom incurable. For a while, the mind may be uneasy in its change of position; but it will, at last, adjust itself to circumstances. There is a worm more destructive than that which consumes our health or property. It is the worm of insatiable passion. This turns life into an irritable, discontented dream, with waking starts of more than ordinary loathing, in which the desire often obtrudes on the sickened mind, to be well rid of such an existence. The poor and the laborious have no such temptations; they have no time for such fancies; and it may justly content men with the common ways of common life, if their obscurity gives them shelter from such hallucinations.

Desire that once passes the moderation of nature, is disease; it is worse than any ordinary illness, because it is in the mind. It becomes an inward and rooted malady. A man is thus a victim to his own best advantages. His intellect, active only for transient sensations, finds stability in nothing, because his interest is in nothing which has truth or stability. He may not want appreciation for the excellent in man or nature; but it is surrounded by such an atmosphere of false sentiment, that all its simplicity is lost in distortion and exaggeration. His fancies are perversions; and, therefore, as the healthy realities of creation and society are in necessary opposition to his fancies, creation and society have nothing for him in their orderly operations but annoyances and disappointments. Calm pleasures he cannot even feel, and to his languid sensibilities they have no pungency. Common virtues are to his stimulated imagination only dull proprieties, things that only befit the unideal, but which have no grandeur for souls that have capacity for more lofty soaring. Quiet feelings of esteem, that seek not for fine words, but content themselves with kindly deeds; friendship, that assumes not to be either poetic or impassioned, but that is satisfied to show itself in homely fidelity, in unadorned loyalty, and in that prosaic constancy which holds closely to the object of esteem when many very eloquent in fine speech think it prudent to retire, cannot allay the cravings of his enthusiasm. Regular pursuits are odious; and thus, between the dissatisfaction with what he has had, and the despair for what he would have but cannot, life is a suspense or a torment.

But many, whose circumstances and constitution

place them much nearer to nature, are not always wholly saved from this temper. With all that is substantially needful for a good and enjoyable life, they become weary, and sullen, and fret, and make others and themselves most unhappy ; they are not content, because their wishes are not sound. Those are constantly in the world who seek only pleasure, and who obtain all of it that the world can bestow ; who have it in abundant fullness, and with all its fascinations and refinements. Yet, what have they at last, and what is their end ? The close of no other kind of life admits of fewer consolations. When the lights seem to burn over habitual festivities with a paler glow, and the music is fainter on the ear, that has long been dead upon the heart ; when the beauty and strength, which had once such power, have given place to infirmity and neglect ; when the love of perishable things still continues in its strength, though the interest of possession is gone forever ; elegant and antiquated Epicureans are chillingly compelled to retire from the scene of their gaiety and their worthlessness. What must life be to them after ? What can the life be which has neither conscience nor memory to cheer it ; nor charities to bless it, nor usefulness to entitle it to look for gratitude or regret ? All they ever lived for, is past ; all they ever lived for, was earthly ; all they ever lived for, was selfish ; and all they ever lived for, they see before them withered. Why should they not wish to die? Why! but for the fear of judgment!

I can well conceive, however, of one to whom life is worn out, and whose wish to leave it we can scarcely censure. It is one who has survived his kindred and his companions, and remains alone in the desert of adversity and the world. When those are gone, who would have been a refuge to him in the heat or in the storm; when those are gone, in whom he had treasured up the golden drops of life; what can he else do than pray, and wish, and sigh to be where his treasures are? A man who has grown hoary amidst the graves of his children, who is left behind by departed generations, and is unknown to living ones, who has a home no longer here, may well, without rebuke, use the words of Jonah, and say, "It is better for me to die than to live." And even though his character may not have been what the good approve, he has still our sympathy; and if years have brought him to solitude but not to peace, he needs it all the more.

Many that are scorned elsewhere, have an asylum from contempt among their kindred. When the prodigal, after all his sin, thought on some spot for rest, he looked toward his father's house; and it was a father's tears that first fell upon his neck; it was a father's kiss that first burned on his cheek. There are those, too, who lose all graces but this one which binds them to their kindred, and this is almost the single tie which binds them to their race. Our Lord represents the miserable Dives as lifting up his eyes in hell, and beseeching father Abraham that Lazarus may be allowed to go and admonish his brethren, "lest they also should come into his place of torment." What a joyless exile earth would be to many of us, if we had not affectionate associations to bind us still to hope? And how often should our hope fail, if we did not think that some were near who would judge us more kindly than the stranger, ay, or even more kindly than we judge ourselves? How barren should existence have been, unless it contained some sanctuary, in which the worst could know that once there, he was in security and love!

And thus it is with numbers among the people of earth. They are nothing, or worse than nothing, to those who have only remotely seen them; and yet every thing to those who have lived near them and with them. The good, even though alone, will yet find many to shelter and to love them. But what must he feel who is desolate and unhonored, in sorrow and decay, without companion or comfort in his descent to the valley of the grave! What must he feel in sad retirement, where he may hide his ruin, but cannot efface his memories! What must he feel who, as death and misery are crushing him, looks about for those that were true to him in all his follies and his frailties, but has none of those to meet his eye, — on whom he passionately calls, but calls in vain, to come once more and soothe his latest and his deserted hour!

Much of dissatisfaction with life arises from a doubly false estimate of life. We underrate our own position in it; we overrate the positions of others. Out of this doubly false estimate spring correspondent false contrasts and desires. The man of bodily labor, longs for mental labor; and, contrasted with his own condition, he thinks it one of perfect ease. And yet, with this wish much is often connected that is strange and inconsistent. You will sometimes hear a man whose toil is physical, expatiate, with emphasis, upon the comparative idleness which the man enjoys whose avocation is intellectual. Yet the man who thus expatiates on the scholar's indolence, finds it a painful task to write a simple letter on the plainest incidents of domestic history; not because he wants ability or intelligence, but because the use of his mind in this way is unfamiliar to him.

The fact is, the scholar would have as much reason to dwell on the ease of the farmer, as the farmer on the ease of the scholar; and so he constantly does, and with just as much of falsehood. The scholar contrasts his position falsely with the farmer's by looking from his own confinement to the farmer's exercise. The farmer contrasts his position falsely with that of the scholar, by looking from his own muscular exertion to the scholar's muscular repose. But he heeds not the paleness of the student's cheek, or the glisten of his eye, which shows that his retreat has been no fair Elysian bower. He heeds not the anxieties, the fears, the leaden hours of prolonged exertion which the library door shuts in. The man of private life desires the distinctions of public office; but he thinks of its power, separate from its toils; of its splendor, separate from its dangers; of the glory of success, separate from the shame of defeat; and of the brilliancy of its outward show, separate from the gnawings of its concealed vexations. He sees not these agitated hours that are hidden from the world; and he feels not these troubles that, though never uttered, cause the sick heart to heave with uneasy palpitations. He does not consider that to widen a man's relations is frequently to multiply his enemies; that to place him in a state which many desire to obtain, is to place him in a position which many will endeavor to embarrass, which many will endeavor to render miserable; that it is to place him in a position exposed to envy, jealousy, misrepresentation, and strife; and that all the torments will haunt it which it is in the power of ambitious rivalry or disappointed competition to invoke.

These things, I am aware, have been said thousands of times before, they will be said thousands of times again; for though life changes in many things as man grows older in history, yet, in many things, life is but the repetition of itself. These things, it may be said, are truisms, an old story; and so they are; but life also is a truism, an old story. The statement of these mistakes is old, but they are in individuals the occasions of a practical waste of life that is ever varied, and is ever new. By underrating, for instance, our own position, we want that spring of hope which is the inspiration of success, and we work in it with feeble and despondent souls. We never come to understand the resources it contained, and therefore we never draw out from them the riches which they might have yielded. By over-rating the position that is *not* ours, our thoughts are divided, and our efforts are unsteady. We do not labor with all our heart and strength in our assigned vocation; and frequently we are induced to leave it, to lose all the power which we expended in it, to begin awkwardly in a new direction, to compete with rivalry in ways for which we were not trained; and thus, doubly wasted, doubly impoverished, we fail of all, and, in the end, grumble with our lot, and quarrel with our life.

And here, again, I will venture another common-place, one as old as moral thought, as old as moral speech. Take a certain level of comfortable existence to begin with, and life from that is equal in all essentials. All poetry, song, drama, fiction, and religion, imply this. The passions are the same; the same in their experience, the same in their results. Take the *woman* that is within the queen, and her love, in its happiness or misery, differs in nothing from that of the girl that waits upon her waiting-woman. The rapture of the girl is, of the two, greater than hers, because it is more natural; and the sadness of a queen afflicted in her *real woman's* heart, would find no magic in the sceptre to heal the wound. Parents on the throne have no more joy in their children than parents in any station, who can meet the demand that health, knowledge, and virtue make for domestic peace. The rich man's pain is not less acute than the poor man's, and remedies are not likely to find it as easily removable.

The deep tragic sorrows that stir the soul, that darken the breast, that cloud the sun, and cover up the world in shroud, though different in form, are of equal force in the extremes of condition. The great lady does not weep with a more hopeless spirit, when she hears that her gallant lord has fallen in battle, than does the poor young wife for her soldier-spouse; and the proud owners of a castle do not bend in more overwhelmed prostration, when the son of their affections and the heir of their splendor is taken to his narrow house, than do the lowly couple of a cottage, when the green sod is laid upon what remains of him that was the light of their hearts, the pride of their life, the staff of their age, their handsome and their stalwart boy. All that makes the essence of life is equal; and the proof, if any were required, may be put into one short sentence: The grief or the enjoyment that reaches life, makes nothing of station; and in the full experience of that grief or enjoyment, no one is conscious of station.

But if it were not even so, yet complaint against life would be against wisdom, against virtue, against religion. Where is the wisdom of that man who murmurs at that which he could not avoid or could not have changed? Where is the virtue of that man on whom blessings are showered in vain, and who has nothing but repining to return for goodness? Where is the virtue of that man, who is ever at secret variance with himself, his condition, his fellows, and his Maker, — who is ever saying, in his bosom's council-chamber, into which he summons his Creator, — Why hast thou thus dealt with me? Where is that man's piety, who, buried in the dungeon of his dark memory, lives amidst the ghosts of his cares, and writes lamentations in the ashes of his burned-out pleasures? Who cannot get to the broad universe around him, range in the liberty of nature, catch the gales that sport with the waters and the woods, and rejoice in the great and good Father who made all things so fair? Where is the piety of that man, to whom the instructions of the gospel, and the example of Christ, and the magnificence of creation, and the lessons of experience, appeal without success and without impression; and who, despite of forbearing mercy and patient expostulation, is still with the splenetic prophet in his thoughts, and in these rebellious thoughts continues to reiterate, "It is better for me to die than to live?"

There are those who say that they have lost all interest in life. It is to them, and not to life, that poverty comes; for life is ever rich in interest. Life is rich for the senses. Every where we see sights and hear sounds that give pleasure. The field, the tree, the brook, the bird, which the most barren country is not without, are things to stir the heart that is not dead to natural sensibility. Even from the filthiest city lane, we can turn our gaze upward, and there we have the sublime and overhanging sky. But in that filthiest lane there will ever be objects within stretch of hand, that excel in deep interest that arched sky, with the beauty of its starlight or the glory of its sun. Take a ragged child that sweeps the crossing, clean his face, gaze into his eyes, and there, soiled and neglected though it is, you will have the image of Him, who kindled the sun, who spread abroad the stars, who built up the sky.

Life is rich for the affections. This is wealth that increases with its use. It is a strength that mounts higher and higher, which at every advance of elevation takes a wider sweep, and warms as it widens. The love of the child reaches to the parent; it spreads to brothers, sisters, and companions. But while the parent's love to the child is such as child never can return, it is a love that does not exhaust itself in the child; it spreads from family to friend, from friends to mankind, and from the household hearth to the infinite and eternal heights of heaven.

Life is rich for the moral sentiments. There are mysteries and complexities of character; there are meanings of events; there are indications of coming results; there are the effects of the Past in the Present, and in the Present also the causes of the Future; there are the workings of Humanity in History; there are the foreshowings of Providence in Prophecy; and these can stimulate all that is meditative and profound within us. Withal, we have the excitement of theories, plans, speculations, efforts, hopes, ideas, achievements, that pant, and speak, and act, with the exhilaration of passion, eloquence, zeal, in devotion, imagination, and doing.

Life has affecting interest for sympathy. We live in the midst of the dying. We laugh in the midst of the despairing. Be where life has least to suffer, and in any space which holds a dense population, we can scarcely take many paces without passing an afflicted heart. Say nothing on the great wrongs of the world; wrongs so huge as to defy expression, yet so common as not to provoke remark, every dwelling has its skeleton, every spirit has its woe, every unwritten life has incidents which the most intimate cannot interpret; it has memories of trouble which the kindest cannot feel.

If a man has clear views of God and of his Providence, if he has a trustful and patient spirit, he will be grateful for his enjoyments, and he will meekly bear his griefs. He will try to extract from his circumstances all the good which they yield him; and he will not darken his position with imaginary calamities. Experience will convince him that he might be more unhappy, and humility will suggest that he has, on the whole, more pleasure than he merits. In the worst trials, faith will teach him that earth is not his rest, that his afflictions here, light and enduring but for a moment, working for him an eternal weight of glory, are but as hasty April showers, that usher in an everlasting summer. Let him be benevolently and usefully active; let him not be indifferent or indolent; let him be interested in all around him, in his family, his neighbors, the world; let him have the goodness of social affection and the zeal of public principle; let him be thus a benefactor to his brethren, and he will be preëminently a benefactor to himself. If he is open to the tribulation of others, he will think less upon his own grievances; and every step that leads him to console real sorrows, will bear him away from fancied ones.

The day of life spent in honest and benevolent labor, comes in hope to an evening calm and lovely; and though the sun declines, the shadows that he leaves behind, are only to curtain the spirit into rest. Earth, and all that it inherits, is to each of us but as the gourd of Jonah. Happy, happy for each, if, at the close of his journey, he can say, not in a querulous discontent, but in believing trust, "It is better for me to die than to live;" or rather, if he can say in the tranquil joyfulness of old Simeon, "Lord, now lettest thou thy servant depart in peace."

MYSTERY IN RELIGION AND IN LIFE.

1 Cor. xiii. 12.

NOW WE SEE THROUGH A GLASS DARKLY.

We see through a glass darkly, we see darkly, but we *see*. We do not see clearly to a great distance, but near at hand, we may discern our way with sufficient distinctness to guide our feet in the paths of peace. Some person has said, that were mystery begins religion ends. This is a pointed sentence, but it is a pointed falsehood. Mystery, in fact, begins not with religion merely, — it begins with life; and it will not end, but with religion and with life. And reason goes hand in hand with mystery. The light of reason ever gleams on the margin of an unmeasured and immeasurable ocean of mystery; and however far we push our discoveries, the line of light only moves on, and has infinite and unfathomable darkness beyond it. Reason and mystery are equally conditions of a spiritual, but limited existence, and indeed, without reason, there could be neither mystery nor religion.

Efforts have been made to exalt revelation on the ruins of reason, but these efforts are perilous to all religion; for if there can be no confidence in reason, there is no foundation for faith. If man has not within him a light of primitive truth, a faculty of spiritual apprehension, to what could a revelation be made? What could heaven appeal to in this dumb, dark silence? What could its prodigies arouse? What could its voice awaken? In vain the dead might start from their graves, in vain might the mountains tremble, and the ocean yawn; it would be as fruitless of spiritual import where there was no spiritual faculty, as the shriekings of Baal's ministers were upon their God on the summit of Mount Carmel.

But every exertion understaken for the religious exaltation of man, supposes faculties in him which can be spiritually influenced; and if it were not so, missions to the idolator or the savage would be the most absurd of speculations; indeed, if it were not so, there would be none to undertake the missions, and none even to conceive them. If man had not that spiritual nature, of which reason is the life, what spiritual idea could be revealed to him? Could the idea of a God be communicated, if the soul had not in itself the elements of that idea? Could the idea of immortality, or of duty? Surely not. If any should suppose they could, why then not try to impress them on inferior creatures? Man therefore may be the subject of revelation, not to make him a religious being, but because he *is* a religious being.

Before we can infer the fact of a revelation, we infer the existence of a God; for it is plain that, to conceive of a revelation from God, it is implied that we conceive of a God from whom the revelation comes. We infer, also, in some degree, the moral perfection of God's character; for, if we did not believe God supremely wise, his revelation would not secure our esteem, and unless we believe Him supremely good, it would not have our trust. Here, now, are most solemn principles with which reason must deal independently; principles, which in the order of logic and of thought, at least, precede revelation, and without admitting which, there can be no intelligent apprehension of revelation.

But the office of reason does not cease here. When any saying or document assumes the claim of a divine revelation, reason has to examine the evidence. The evidence is either historical or moral; in theological phraseology, either external or internal. Reason must judge in either case. No other judge can be; for the matter under consideration cannot be a judge for itself. Reason must examine the external evidence; must ascertain whether the facts averred, natural or supernatural, actually occurred; whether the testimony adduced is sufficient; whether, if the facts did occur, they adequately sustain the doctrine asserted. You cannot exclude reason from the domain of historical evidence; neither can you from that of moral evidence. An intellectual contradiction cannot come from God; and reason in this case is an immediate and a final authority. All admit this. Men may dispute whether a proposition *is* an intellectual contradiction; but once being so determined, there is no discussion. A miracle, if such were exhibited, could not force conviction; after ten thousand miracles, the inherent falsehood would be unchanged. And the moral is subjected to the test of reason as well as the intellectual.

We often hear it advanced in favor of Christianity, that its doctrines are worthy of God. Such an assertion assumes that we have some knowledge of what is, or what is not, worthy of God. Whence have we this knowledge? From revelation? If so, we cannot use it for evidence of revelation. If it can be fairly used as such, then is it independent of revelation. When we say, then, of doctrines, that they are worthy of God, we place confidence in the rectitude of our moral sense. We hold that it has a true relation to God, and has a true perception of what is contrary to his excellence, or in accordance with it. There may, then, be a moral contradiction as well as an intellectual one, and with the same influence upon conviction. There must be first principles of right as well as of truth, and we must be capable of knowing them. Nor can we suppose them changed when applied to the character or actions of God; else we could not understand what was worthy of him or otherwise, and then all our sayings on the point were without meaning and without value. A doctrine which should shock our moral sense would, on these grounds, be rejected, whatever authority it claimed. A contradiction to the first principles of right would involve a self-evident condemnation, however boldly it was announced from God; it would bear in its own statement the spirit of a lie; and no mystery could shield it, and no miracle uphold it.

Granting the revelation to be recorded in written documents, and these documents authenticated, reason then must be exercised in their interpretation. What was their character, was the question hitherto; what is their import, is the question now. This or the other must be resolved by examination. I do not say by whom, or by how many, whether by councils or individuals; but, by whomsoever it is done, the process is intellectual; it is a work of human reason. Whatever laws pertain to the interpretation of secular records, are those which equally pertain to the interpretation of sacred documents. To both we must apply the analysis of antiquity, the analogies of history, the results of criticism.

Nor do the primitive laws of intellect and conscience, by which we test the character of an assumed revelation, cease to be operative when we come to test the meaning of an admitted one. If an assertion contradict the plain dictates of reason, that is no meaning from the mind of God. If an assertion contradict the clear voice of conscience, that can be no meaning from the mind of God. The admission of a revelation does not abrogate the laws of thought or duty, for they are immutable; and a true revelation must tend to exalt, not to subvert them. Moreover, they are the only means which men possess by which to judge interpretation. Few have much acquaintance with history; fewer still can interrogate antiquity; and the number is considerably small, indeed, who are adepts in the philosophy of criticism; but all, if they will be just to them, have the moral sense, and common sense.

If a doctrine, then, is proposed to an unlearned but sound minded man as a doctrine sustained by the word of God, is he not justified in bringing it to the test of his reason? Must he not be aware that his reason certainly is from God, and given to him for his highest destiny? Must he not be aware that, in fundamental principles, it is the same in all nations and in every age, however speech may vary and customs may change? Must he not have the like strong confidence in his conscience? If the doctrine be against these, he has authority to pronounce it false. If an interpretation is advanced which he cannot refute, may he not consistently and humbly answer: "I am not skilled in dialects, I am not intimate with history, remoter times I have never explored, with philosophy I am unacquainted; but by the light which the Creator has bestowed on every man whom he sends into the world, your saying appears to me a falsehood, and I do not believe that a God of truth has revealed it." What other test than this have men in general? And if you deprive them of it, nearly the whole mass must be given over to a blind submission. Will it be objected that reason is here made ultimate and supreme?

It may be so; it must be so. Hold what belief we will; take what form of religion we choose; no matter what ideas we have on the standard of doctrine, on the nature or the extent of individual judgment or church authority; no matter what we conceive to be the appointed mode of dispensing truth or ending controversies; it does not signify whether on these subjects we maintain the widest freedom or the most complete obedience; so long as we maintain any faith as intelligent beings, the basis on which we rest it all is reason.

This is a thing not of our power, or our choice; it is a necessity of our creation, — a necessity, indeed, in the constitution of the spiritual universe.

And from what stage in the course that I have sketched will you exclude reason? Will you exclude it from finding out the meanings of the Book? If a Protestant, you then violate the first principles of your Protestantism; or you must deny that the process of interpretation is in any sense a work of reason. If a Catholic, you have no means to prove the authority of your church, which you hold to be a divine institution, and which revelation only can establish. Will you exclude it from examining the evidence by which the Bible can be shown to contain divine communications? Then you take away the foundation of revealed religion altogether. Will you exclude it from our convictions concerning the existence and character of God? Then you destroy all religion, whether natural or revealed, whether innate or derived, whether intuitive or historical.

But, if you will do none of these things, I claim, then, no more for reason than you must allow; I claim only for reason, that which cannot be denied without a denial, virtually, of all truth, all certainty; without a denial, in fact, which would cast us, at once, on the dark, desolate, trackless, and boundless ocean of universal scepticism.

Do we then put away mystery from religion? By no means. Religion, as I have said, is in the midst of mystery. Our existence is in the midst of mystery. Mystery is omnipresent. But mystery does not surely exclude all definite knowledge; nay, it is by means of definite knowledge, even that we think of mystery. It is by limited space, that we apprehend the unlimited; by time, we conceive of eternity; by a consciousness of dependent being, we rise to an idea of that which is infinite and perfect. We do not, as it is at times asserted, by this mode of argument bring God to the bar of our fallible judgment, and try his word by the dictates of our own proud will. No; most certainly, we do not. We do not presume to know all that belongs to God; we would only judge what claims to be of God, by the light with which he has gifted us. By what we understand of God, we would test that which claims his authority, and this is not only consistent with humility, but it is commanded by duty.

The being of God is not measurable, but it is intelligible; the character of God is inscrutable, but it is not inconsistent. It were impious to disbelieve a word of God, but not so to doubt whether when men insist on it, they speak this word, or understand it. Convince me that what is written is this word, and I submit, with my spirit and my understanding; convince me that an interpretation is this word, and I believe; and of necessity, I cannot but believe. I reject no doctrine because it involves mystery. Mysteriousness is to me, in itself, no objection to a doctrine. I reject no doctrine for want of plainness, but want of proof.

Mystery is, I have admitted, a necessary element in religion; and if I reject religion on the ground of mystery, on the same ground I must deny all existence; I must deny my own existence. But I do not accept either the plea of mystery or that of intelligibleness, as an argument for truth. A proposition may be equally false, whether it be hard to be understood, or easy. I do not reject a doctrine because I cannot fully comprehend it, but in that which I may have knowledge, I ask for evidence. Herein, I obey the apostolic injunction, — "Try the spirits whether they are of God, because many false prophets are gone out into the world." For this reason, he tells the disciples to "believe not every spirit." What spirit, then, they would receive, that spirit they must try, and this trial must decide on its character, whether it was, or was not, of God.

The maintenance of reason, is, therefore, no denial of mystery. In every object which has relation to religious ideas or religious sentiments there is mystery.

There is mystery in God. Who can find out the Almighty to perfection? Mysterious with infinite sacredness is that awful Being, from whom all things have sprung; mysterious in his omnipotence, with which volition is creation, and creation is boundless; mysterious in his wisdom, which has designed and accomplished the grand economy of being, which has adjusted all its contrivances for the security of harmony and happiness, which has given a purpose to every atom of matter and to every pulse of life, and which permits no atom and no pulse to fail in the purpose whereunto it is appointed; mysterious in his goodness, which ever communicates and never needs to receive, which is gentle without weakness, and merciful without emotion; mysterious in his essence, shrouded in darkness, silent and unapproachable; every where present, yet having no place; eternal in duration, yet related to no time.

There is mystery in the universe. There is mystery in its age. What is the life of man amidst those old worlds? When did they begin to exist? What changes have they passed through? What convulsions and revolutions have occurred in the empires of space? There is mystery in their vastness. Already the certain discoveries of science have outrun the dreams of fancy, and reason walks securely over fields of immensity, where imagination grows feeble and bewildered. But, even beyond the ken of reason, what unknown labyrinths, what regions of existence and of light, what untravelled deserts in the kingdoms of our God. There is mystery in the laws of the universe. How are worlds held to their centres? Whence their motion? Whence their immutable regularity? There is mystery in the construction of the universe. We know not of it; it is hidden from us. We do not understand a blade of grass, the leaf of a flower, and the unseen millions that live on it. We need not go widely into space for things beyond our knowledge; the globe on which we tread suffices. A grain of sand, a gleam of fire, a breath of air, mocks our intelligence, and defies our wisdom. Afar off, there are wilds unknown, and near us are things inscrutable. We live in the midst of infinite existence, and widely as we can see, and vastly as we have discovered, we have but crossed the threshold, we have but entered the vestibule of the Creator's temple. In this temple there is an everlasting worship of life, an anthem of many choruses, a hymn of incense that goes up forever.

The universe is full of world-dramas. If this earth, where man abides, has had such a history, if it has had such strange vicissitudes, what marvels may belong to every spot in illuminated space! Faintly can we dream of the life that animates the systems of creation, the happiness that blesses them, and the beauty that adorns them! And this sublime mysteriousness does not fall barren on us, if we have devout hearts. It humbles, while it exalts us; and, while in the sense of our littleness, we bow our heads to the dust, with solemn adoration, also, we lift our souls to God. From darkness have all these come at the bidding of Almighty will; they exist by Almighty power; they manifest Almighty goodness; they are the spheres of Almighty purposes; and when we gaze upon this fair creation, in its bounty around our feet, and in its splendor above our heads, with the Psalmist we exclaim, "O Lord how manifold are thy works, in wisdom thou hast made them all!"

When, therefore, we consider the earth, which is but God's footstool, and the heavens, which are but the work of his fingers, we ask, What is man, that God is mindful of him, and the son of man, that God should visit him? But man is greater than the earth, and greater than the heavens; and man, too, is more a mystery than the earth, and more a mystery than the heavens. Man is a mystery in the marvellous formation of his body; but, more profoundly, he is a mystery in the union of that body with a soul. We know this bond, and we feel it, but we cannot explain it. There is that within us which is active, joined to that which is inert; there is that within us which can think, joined to that which, by its own nature, is insensible; and that whose proper tendency is dissolution and division, is joined to that whose very essence is unity.

Man is a mystery in the union he exhibits of progress and decay in his earthly life. "I die daily," says the apostle. There is a sense in which we live daily, in which we die daily. There is physical progression, there is physical decay; for one period a daily physical life, for another a daily physical death. Man grows slowly from weakness to independence. Infancy strengthens into childhood; childhood bounds into youth; youth sobers into manhood; manhood softens into age; age totters to its second cradle, and in that it slumbers to the tomb. The life of sensation grows into that of wonder; then come hope and passion; then care and labor; last of all, exhausted experience, and a wish for rest. Every day in the first portion of our course fastens a tie to earth; and in the latter portion of it every day loosens one. For a time, the circle of our relationships in the world enlarges; then comes a period, when this is reversed, and the circle is contracted, our friends pass from the scene, our cotemporaries disappear; we begin literally to feel that earth is no longer our proper place; our life is no longer of it; it has ceased to be our dwelling; and we gaze through hope and tears for habitations which are eternal in the heavens.

Yet, with all this bodily and social decay, there may be a moral growth of mind. The passions subside, and meditation may take the place of impulse; speculation may give way to knowledge, and wisdom succeed to both. Though our bodies waste, and even our intellectual energy decay, the spiritual man may be renewed, the sight of the soul may be more clear, and the voice of conscience more distinct; the inward nature is then governed by ideas, rather than instincts; its inspiration is from faith rather than desire; and its visions are formed in the light of hope, rather than in the mists of pleasure.

Man is a mystery in his grandeur and his baseness. The intellectual grandeur of man is evidenced in an ever-productive genius, which seems quickened from the creativeness of God; the moral grandeur of man has been evidenced in a magnitude of worth which seemed replenished from the heart of God's grace. But notwithstanding this intellectual and this moral grandeur, great has been human folly, and great has been human guilt. Man has bent to the most insane absurdities; he has given himself to the grossest errors; he has taken the most wretched chimeras for truth, and the basest idolatries for religion. He, too, who has been capable of such godlike generosity, has been most vilely selfish; he who has shown the mercy of heaven, has exhibited the malignity of hell; and he who has risen to the loftiest sentiments, has also sunk to the worst of passions. Humanity has united, in most marvellous contradiction, the majesty of reason and the supremacy of conscience with the vanity of desire and the frailty of will.

If man be thus a mystery in his present life, much more he is a mystery in death, and in the immortality to which death translates him. O what a veil conceals that passage from our senses. Death is certain, and it is silent. We walk upon a grave, and the clay of mouldered generations on which we tread has neither sound nor voice. Our hearts are now active with many desires; ere long, their chords will melt into ashes. We enter a festive room, bridal, or baptismal; faces are glad, and lights are brilliant; but soon these faces will vanish from earth, even as the lights die upon the finished banquet.

The sublimest spectacle which the world offers, are men in their thousands and their might. Grand, though with melancholy grandeur, is an army with banners, an array of martial manhood in its courage and its prime, treading to the note that pierces the ear, and that swells the heart; yet, in the most potent host which the sun ever saw collected, he would not have accomplished many revolutions, when there would be few ears to listen and few hearts to bound.

Death is silent. In the city, while men are brawling and busy in the crowded street, death is entering the secret chambers, and friends sit pallid by the couches of the breathless, or love is drinking in the sigh which bears the soul to heaven. Death is silent; those whose very looks spoke to us in life, pass from our sight as the shadow from the dial, and the music of their words become sad echoes in the distance of our memory. Death is silent. Living hatred thunders in the strife of war, but when the contest is over, Death, grim and speechless, is monarch of the field. Death is silent. Tempests shriek madly upon ocean, and many are they who sink with this requiem into their fathomless grave; but from the depths of that sublime sepulchre, no sound comes back to tell of those who perished. Death is silent, yet not so entirely; silent it is to the ear, but not always to the heart; our brethren are still bound to us, and though dead, they have not ceased to be. There is much to be felt and learned where they rest.

Humility has instruction from the proud man's

monument, and content a lesson from the vanity that overlies his clay. There is pathos in the solitude where the stranger sleeps; there is mute eloquence on his unlettered grave; there is beauty in the poor man's epitaph, inscribed honestly by affection; there is sublimity in the rude sculpture of the peasant's tomb, when it is the effort to symbolize an immortal faith. And it is such faith which takes terror from the power of death, and despair from the silence of the grave. There is that in us which is not all clay. That which belongs to earth, must go to earth; but when earth claims and gets back its atoms, God gathers up and calls home his spirits.

More prolific is the Creative Power in minds than in matter, and the universe is more filled with souls than with worlds. Within every human form there is an existence destined for eternal relations and eternal progress. While my senses rest upon the mortal, my faith tells me of the immortal. If I lean over the couch of my last earthly friend, I may weep, but I will not despair If I see the aged fall in the ripeness of their years, and the young cut down in the fullness of their prime, I shall consider the difference nothing in the birth of endless being. When I behold the man of great and developed powers levelled with the least of his brethren, the speculation of a godlike reason extinguished in the eye, the ecstasy of a sublime imagination palsied in the breast, I do not lose my confidence; I am persuaded of a sphere beyond the present, where this reason may seek for loftier truth, and this imagination steep itself in diviner beauty.

And this persuasion has full confirmation in Jesus, the mystery; but yet more, the miracle of humanity. The miracle of humanity! By what designation more appropriate shall we describe the Saviour? He that rose upon the age with a goodness which nothing in the age inspired; he that loved with the fullness and the impartiality of Heaven, when souls were stern and hearts contracted; he that cared only for the sanctification of man's spirit where others cared merely for the observance of the letter; he that spoke as none had ever spoken, yet whose words were plain to childhood; he that looked on guilt with deepest abhorrence, yet beheld the sinner with divine compassion; he that ever lived in converse with the unseen, yet walked among his brethren in all gentle and affectionate offices; he that knew the secret of the grave, yet cast no shadow on the cheerfulness of life; he that had excellence so endearing that we feel him to be our brother, yet so perfect, that while it stimulates our loftiest exertions, it infinitely and forever transcends them.

Mystery! we need not ascend above the skies, or go into the grave for mystery! The world of human life has mysteries impenetrable, and Divine Providence sustains an agency before our eyes which hourly rebukes our vain sagacity. Genius walks by the side of the witless; the one rejoices in the splendor of a God; the other has a consciousness that merely lives. Knowledge with a memory enriched from the treasures of the past, knowledge glorious with the spoils of time and thought, sojourns beside ignorance that gropes in beamless night. Wealth, that has no stores to hold its fullness, is but a span from poverty that has no inheritance but the grave. Luxury that sickens with its pomp, is within sight of destitution which grows pale with famine. The merry peals of enraptured laughter stir the same atmosphere which sobs with the complainings of the poor, which is thickened by the tears of the wretched. Systems of existence only a little apart, there are every where, that have but infrequent interchange and but imperfect sympathy. Still, though they have many points of difference, they have, also, both in compensation and suffering, much in common. Death comes to all; it pulls down the pride of the mighty, and it gives the weary rest. The ungifted miss the ecstasy of genius, but they are saved from its penalties. The unlearned have not the delights of knowledge, neither have they its responsibilities. In the depths of toil and poverty, are the kindred of home, the light of its affectionate instincts, the intercourse of its blessed sympathies.

Much that is most exquisite in humanity, is independent on condition. Enough of good there is in the lowest estate to sweeten life; enough of evil in the highest to check presumption; enough there is of both in all estates, to bind us in compassionate brotherhood, to teach us impressively that we are of one dying and one immortal family. These inequalities, so striking in our temporary pilgrimage, are nothing to our progrssive soul; they are harsh to the eye of sense, but they vanish in the light of faith; they are only shadows in this our dawn of being, that melt away in the clear day of eternity.